Salem

Maritime Salem in the Age of Sail

D0441640

Produced by the
National Park Service, Division of Publications
for Salem Maritime National Historic Site

In cooperation with the Peabody Museum
and the Essex Institute, Salem, Massachusetts

U.S. Department of the Interior
Washington, D.C. 1987

3 1215 00089 5562

In the years following the American Revolution, sailing vessels from Salem opened new markets to American trade from Bordeaux to Sumatra. In its peak years between 1790 and 1807 the port was identified with the Eastern luxuries trade, as tea, coffee, pepper, and other goods made the port one of the most prosperous cities in America. *Salem* is a history of the port's seafaring era and a guide to the Salem institutions that preserve its maritime heritage. The introduction recalls the vitality of the port. The main narrative in Section 2, based on a text by K. David Goss of the Essex Institute, documents the port's rise and decline and looks in some detail at the merchants, crews, ships, and Salem's world trade network. A guide to the historic maritime sites of Salem is provided in Section 3.

The publication of this book was made possible in part by a grant from the Eastern National Parks and Monuments Association.

National Park Handbooks, compact introductions to the natural and historical places administered by the National Park Service, are published to promote public understanding and enjoyment of the parks. Each handbook is intended to be informative reading and a useful guide to park features. More than 100 titles are in print. They are sold at parks and can be purchased by mail from the Superintendent of Documents, U.S. Government Printing Office, Washington D.C. 20402.

Library of Congress Cataloging in Publication Data
Salem: A History for Salem Maritime National
Historic Site, Massachusetts
Produced by the National Park Service, Division of Publications in cooperation with the Peabody Museum and the Essex Institute, Salem, Massachusetts.
(National Park Handbook; 126)
Bibliography: p.   Includes index.
1. Salem (Mass.)—History. 2. Salem (Mass.)—
Commerce. 3. Salem Maritime National Historic Site
(Mass.)—Guidebooks. I. United States. National
Park Service. Division of Publications. II. Peabody
Museum of Salem. III. Essex Institute.
F74.S1S28 1987   974.4'5   85-21545
ISBN 0-912627-30-1

Contents

Part 1

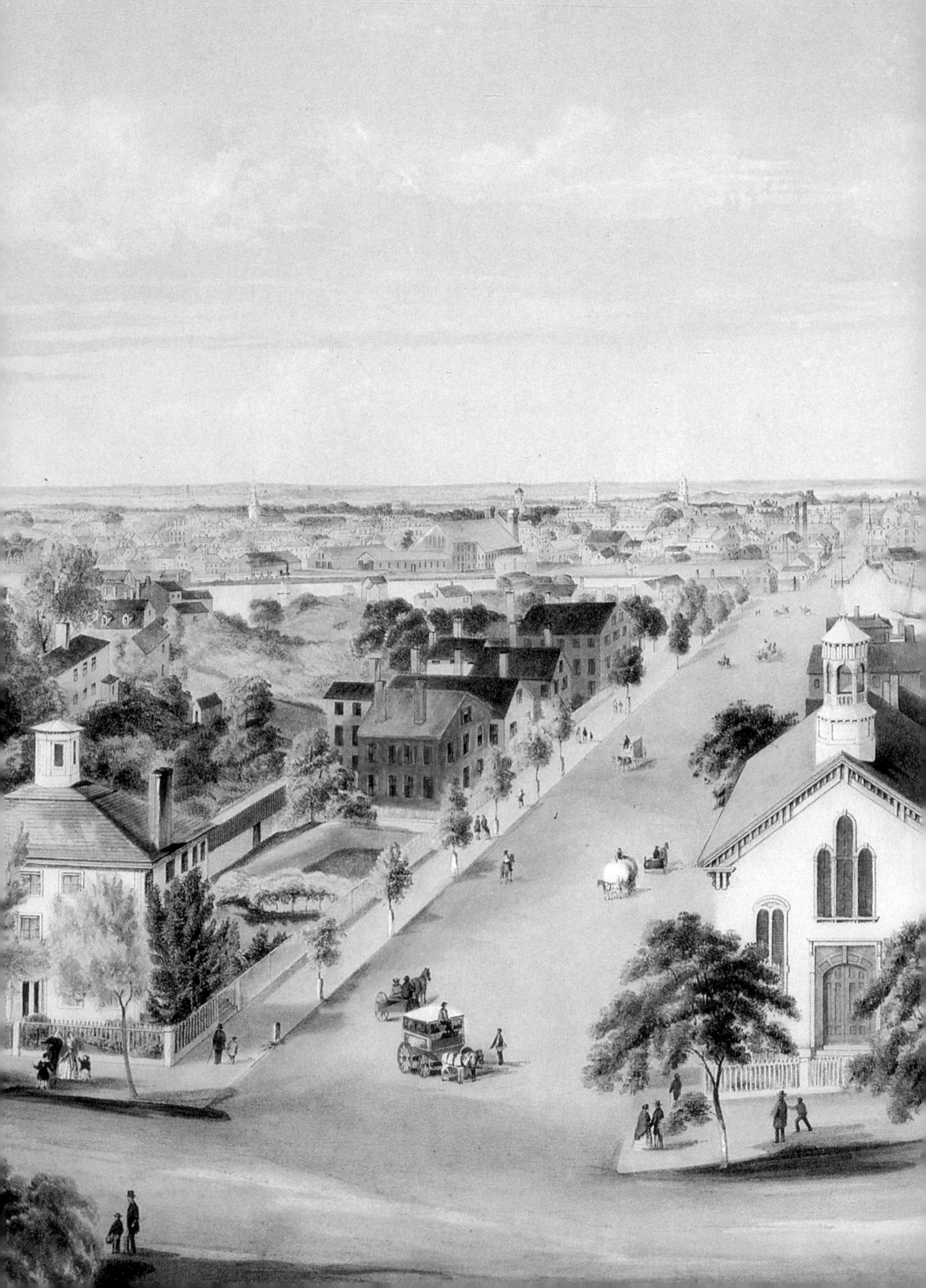

The City Sea Trade Built

From the window of his Custom House office, Surveyor Nathaniel Hawthorne commanded a view of Derby Wharf. There was no lighthouse in his day, and the wharf would have been lined with warehouses.

Pages 4-5: *Salem as it appeared in 1852, looking north on Lafayette Street across wharf-crowded South River. Derby Wharf, the longest in Salem, is seen at far right. Near the wharf, the Custom House, Hawkes House, and Derby House* **(pages 8-9)** *overlooked the heart of the waterfront.*

Roam the streets of Salem for a few hours and two qualities will make themselves felt. At every turn you catch a glimpse of water, for so long the port's lifeblood. Almost as palpable is the sense of history—a strong presence in a port over 350 years old. To walk the stark length of Derby Wharf when fog moves over the water like a dream of the past is to sense the time when Salem was a vital conduit of America's Indies trade.

It is easy to conjure up the Salem that flourished after the Revolution, for the city was shaped by the sea, and though the flood-tide of maritime commerce long ago receded, the high-water marks are indelible. Before South River was filled in, the inner harbor extended deep into town. One can stand before buildings, now surrounded by urban activity, that were once immersed in the industry of the waterfront. The few wharves that remain, now stripped of their clutter and noise, represent the many that reached into Salem harbor to receive commercial vessels.

The vessels long ago sank or rotted, but the grand houses built by their owners give the port an elegance undiminished today. Chestnut Street, with its row of imposing yet restrained Federal-style houses, is one of the most architecturally significant avenues in America. Palladian doorways, with finely glazed fanlights and sidelights, illuminate the halls with the light of a calmer and more measured day. A delicate balance of orient and occident characterizes the high-ceilinged rooms. Chinese wallpaper harmonizes with Chippendale chairs, betokening Salem's long and fruitful association with the East.

Close by these houses, many of which are still private, are three public institutions that keep alive Salem's seafaring heritage. Since 1799, Salem's merchants, captains, and seamen's descendents have been depositing the art and artifacts of maritime commerce in the Peabody Museum. Its galleries portray their ships and boats, the tools of their trade, and the goods and curiosities they brought home. The Essex Institute's collections of paintings, drawings, and household items provide a close look at domestic life in early Essex County. Both have extensive collections of ship's logs and journals that record the thoughts and feelings of those who went to sea. Salem Maritime National Historic Site is a

piece of Salem as it was—the wharves and the structures that inevitably grew nearby: merchants' houses, warehouses, a store, and the Custom House.

Perhaps the past so pervades Salem's streets because the city was built on one of our oldest and most basic endeavors: pulling staple goods from the sea and finding routes over its surface by which to trade them. The traders and sailors who walked these streets were among the craftiest practitioners of their calling. As the British consul noted in 1789, "The inhabitants of New England may be said to be a peculiar people; they have more public spirit, more enterprize, energy and activity of mind and body than their neighbors."

How did the "Yankee Trader" get that way? To what do we attribute his industry, his resilience, his special relationship with the sea? New England's hilly land and thin, stony soil would not yield the staple cash crops of the southern colonies, but it offered broad natural harbors, seemingly endless forests, and tumbling rivers to power mills. The resourceful settlers turned the forests into ships and boats and took their harvest from the sea. A seafaring culture took root along the length of the New England coast, and out of it came a "codfish aristocracy" quite different from the planters to the south.

Salem's early fishermen and great merchants epitomized the New England trader. They possessed an acute business sense, but were not overly cautious men. They brought to their livelihood an attitude that went beyond mere getting and spending. One observer characterized them as "distinguished by a lively imagination . . . Their enterprises are sudden, bold, and sometimes rash. A general spirit of adventure prevails here."

Sea trade was indeed a colorful and fascinating way to earn one's bread. Salem's harbor was alive with sail—skiffs taking customs officials out to anchored vessels, sloops heading for the fishing banks off Cape Cod, coasting schooners carrying cod to Charleston and bringing timber from Maine, and three-masted Indiamen returning with exotic goods from ports in the Indian Ocean.

The waterfront was a melange of sights, sounds, and odors. The rich sea-smell of the mud flats exposed at low tide mingled with the aromas of spices and rank fumes drifting from the tanneries.

The fine craftsmanship and fluid lines of the central staircase enhance the Derby House entrance hall.

Left: *Merchant Elias Hasket Derby entertained his guests in the parlor, within view of his wharf and warehouses.*

11

Rough warehouses like the one on Central Wharf were common along the waterfront. The goods they held enabled their owners to lavish fine details on their own houses, as seen on the portico of the Gardner-Pingree House.

Right: *Salem's Old Town Hall, on Derby Square, occupies the site of merchant Elias Hasket Derby's mansion. The ground floor marketplace opened in 1816, followed a year later by the second floor town hall.*

Filleted cod dried in ordered rows on hundreds of racks along the shore. From across South River at Briggs' shipyard came the syncopation of broadaxe and caulking hammer.

From what is now Salem's central traffic circle to beyond the House of the Seven Gables, dozens of wharves jutted into river and harbor. Warehouses, ship's chandlers, counting houses, and tradesmen's shops crowded the wharves. The cooper bent hoops around curved staves and sold the cask to a rum merchant. In a sail loft over a warehouse, itinerant sailmakers sewed stitches in a topsail. A block maker fashioned the wood-and-bronze blocks by which a vessel's sails and spars were handled. At the small uncovered ropewalks, straining workers twisted ropes into massive anchor cables.

Derby Street was alive with the ebb and flow of maritime commerce. A shipowner explained to a visiting Indian merchant the intricacies of his vessel's rigging. Nearby a captain recruited seamen for a voyage to the Baltic. A street merchant sold lemons from Spain, while in the West India Goods Store, a captain's wife examined exotic cottons. Merchants struck deals that could take two years to bear fruit. When an East Indiaman completing such a venture was hauled into its berth by wharf workers, the owner came aboard to greet the captain and be apprised of the voyage's outcome. The customs officers carted their great beam scales to the vessel's side. Windlasses driven by men or horses creaked as they lifted bales of cotton, bags of coffee and pepper, and casks of Madeira wine from the hold.

These scenes were replayed countless times during the two centuries Salem was an important American port. This narrative traces the rise of the port from its beginnings as a provincial fishing village to the years when it dominated American trade in the Indian Ocean. Though the focus is on Salem's "Golden Age," between the Revolution and the War of 1812, it also recounts how the people of Salem built on the efforts of those who came before. With the passing decades, each generation bore the deepening legacy of danger and pride left by its predecessors. They failed and they flourished, they died at sea and in bed, and their memory lived to haunt and inspire their children.

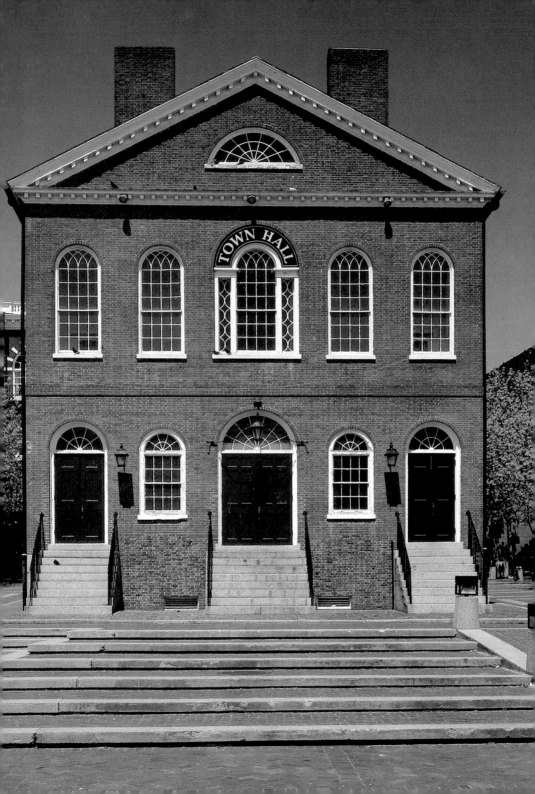

Part 2

"To the Farthest Port of the Rich East"

The Rise of Salem

September 1803. Loaded with coffee and pepper, the ship *Cincinnatus*, six months out of Sumatra, rounds Naugus head and sails slowly into Salem Harbor. A boy at the end of Derby Wharf spies *Cincinnatus'* sails and runs to claim from owner Joseph Peabody his coin for being the first to see the vessel after its 16-month voyage to the East Indies.

The people of Salem never grew jaded by the arrival of an East Indiaman from around the Cape of Good Hope. In the port's busiest years, when scores of sails brightened the harbor and the world's goods crowded its wharves, such a voyage underpinned Salem's prosperity and focused its spirit of community. Since the Revolution the Eastern luxuries trade had become the special province of the port, gaining for it a reputation as the Venice of the New World. The financial and physical risks taken by the merchants and crews made Salem by 1800 the Nation's richest city per capita, with an air of sophistication and worldliness rivaling Boston.

Salem's major role in opening the Eastern trade is only one facet of the city's long and eventful maritime life. From its earliest days, when hungry colonists turned from New England's stony soil to the sea, through the era when virtually every citizen depended on shipping, to the last years when youths looked to Salem's cotton mills rather than its dwindling merchant fleet for work, the port's history is told through its changing relationship with the sea.

Indians were already living on the quiet harbor they called Naumkeag, "the fishing place," when 30 men, women, and children from the failing Dorchester Company fishing station at nearby Cape Ann migrated there in 1626 under the leadership of Roger Conant, a former Plymouth colonist. Living on the shore of the North River in sod-roofed huts and bark-covered wigwams patterned after Indian dwellings, the settlers eked out a living by fishing and trading with the Indians.

Within two years the company's English directors transferred their claim to the New England Company, a group of Puritan entrepreneurs. Congregational Puritans wanted to purify the Church of England of its "popery" and to assert the autonomy of the congregation. Leaving behind the Stuart kings' repression of religious dissent, they intended to set up a model Christian community in the New World, proving that people could live according to the New Testament and still prosper. About 50 settlers sailed on *Abigail* under the leadership of John Endecott.

From the beginning, Salem cast its lot with the sea. In the spring of 1629, as the new settlers planted maize and built thatch-roofed cottages, shipwrights were building fishing shallops. Cod was already becoming crucial to the colony's survival, both as a food staple and as fertilizer. When clergymen arrived that summer, the Puritans formed the first Congregational Society in America and renamed the community Salem (from the Hebrew word Shalom), "the place of peace."

Another group of Puritans took control of the New England Company in 1630 and reorganized it as the Massachusetts Bay Company. That spring John Winthrop, a London attorney chosen to lead the first mass migration from England, arrived at Salem with eleven ships, and before the year was out six more arrived. Sustained by their covenant with God to establish a "city upon a hill," nearly a thousand settlers, mostly Puritan yeoman, tradesmen, and artisans, arrived by Christmas.

Believing that Salem lacked adequate farmland and harbor, Winthrop soon moved the Bay Colony capital a few miles south to Boston. Because the company officers—prosperous men from London's commercial class—moved to New England with their charter, they were virtually independent. The company's corporate organization evolved into a government, which, at least on paper, preserved traditional English rights and liberties. It was far from democratic, however, as a settler had to be a church member to become a voting freeman, and entrance to what historian Louis Wright calls this "aristocracy of the pious" was closed to most people.

Salem held on as a trading post, selling its small surplus of corn, cod, beef, and other provisions to the steady stream of Puritan immigrants. But with its population growing and no easy access to the fertile hinterland, Salem found it more and more difficult to grow enough to feed itself. Economic salvation came by way of the pulpit. Seeing the need for a local industry, 38-year-old Rev. Hugh Peter turned his eye on the humble cod. He organized the haphazard fisheries, promoted the building of a salt works to process dried fish, and helped John Holgrave build a wharf, drying racks, or "flakes," and a tavern on Winter Island. Salem fishermen made more ambitious voyages to the rich fishing banks off Cape Cod and Newfoundland, bringing home halibut, mackerel, haddock, and cod.

The "sacred cod" gave Salem a secure economic base, but when the Great Migration of Puritan settlers began to fall off around 1637, Salem's merchant-captains, left with a surplus, had to expand their markets. They supplemented their catch with timber, shingles, and barrel staves and ventured south in the fall. Sometimes wintering over in Maryland or Virginia, they returned with iron, hides, tallow, salt, horses, cotton, tobacco, and most important, rice, corn, and wheat. The tireless Reverend Peter spurred the shipbuilding industry to build the larger shallops and ketches needed for this trade.

In 1638, the settlement turned out to greet the ship *Desire*, in from the "Caribbee Islands" with a cargo of cotton, tobacco, salt, and slaves—the earliest recorded voyage of a Salem vessel to the West Indies. With these first tentative steps beyond the home market, the way to prosperity became clear. Sugar, produced on the large slave plantations of Barbados, Antigua, and St. Kitts, was the sweet gold that carried New England's early trade. Refined, it yielded the thick, dark molasses that was distilled into rum—a drink with thirsty markets at home, in Europe, and in Africa.

Though the slaves on *Desire* were the first imported to the Bay Colony, they did not become a staple of Salem's trade. The traffic in humans, however, was all too profitable, and some New England ports developed the infamous "Triangular Trade": West Indies sugar and molasses to New England; New England rum to Africa's west coast; and African slaves to West Indies sugar plantations. The hands of most Salem merchants and captains were not dirtied by this dark side of American commerce. They did, though, supply the plantations with "refuse" cod for the slaves, horses to turn the sugar mills, and wooden staves for the molasses casks. They provided a steady market for the sugar, molasses, and indigo produced there. More than a few of the fortunes of New England's post-Revolutionary ruling class were built on the slave plantation supply trade.

Emboldened by their success in the "Sugar Islands," Salem merchants sailed to Nova Scotia and Bermuda and struck out across the Atlantic. In the Netherlands, Channel Islands, and British Isles, they traded lumber, hides, masts, wool, and their best rum for salt, linen, hardware, bar iron, and bills of exchange. From southern France, the Iberian peninsula, and the Wine Islands (Madeira, Azores, Canaries), they obtained wine, hides, fruit, and Spanish pieces of eight in return for their best cod, called "dunfish," tobacco, and pipe staves for the vintners.

The West Indies trade became even more lucrative when the British Navigation Acts of 1660 and 1663 gave Americans a virtual monopoly of shipping between the mainland colonies and the West Indies. This trade became the axis of New England commerce and Salem's mainstay until the Revolution. Salem merchants quickly learned the tricks of the trade, such as occasionally stopping for cheaper sugar at a French West Indies island, a practice outlawed by the trade acts. They established early the Salem tradition of dealing in profitable but risky cargoes such as sugar, the price for which was notoriously unstable. Their boldness paid off. Less than 30 years after the fishing industry was established, John Josselyn, a widely-traveled English adventurer not easily impressed, remarked on the "very rich merchants" he met in Salem.

These were tough traders who built and sailed the ships they owned, buttressed by the Puritan virtues of thrift, sobriety, and honest dealing. Their religion promoted a convenient marriage of profits and piety. They thrived under the belief that hard work glorified God and, if wealth resulted, that was a sign of His favor. Most prominent among the early merchants was Philip English, who arrived in the 1660s from the Isle of Jersey. At one point he owned wholly or in part 20 vessels, sailing to Barbados, Newfoundland, Surinam, and his home Channel

Islands. Capt. John Turner died at 36, but in his short time he owned several ships, made a fortune in the Barbados trade, and built the later-famous house with seven gables near his wharf. Roger Derby rose from soap boiler to minor merchant and was progenitor of Salem's most famous merchant family. As shipowners like English and Turner brought more goods and money into the fishing village, they gained prominence and influence, although the magistrates and clergy remained atop Salem's political and social structure in the 17th century.

By the end of the century dozens of vessels were sailing out of the harbor, mostly fishing ketches of less than 40 tons. There were few wharves, and at low tide the vessels rested askew on the exposed mud flats. On the flat neck of land where the village had grown, the plain meeting house dominated the group of warehouses, shops, and steep-roofed dwellings. New arrivals had to adapt quickly to bitter New England winters and the constant threat of smallpox. It was a quiet town, but hardly sleepy, for the inhabitants had little choice but to be industrious. They were living on the margin, and everyone's attention was devoted to the critical business of sending out vessels to bring back fish. Not only did the town's commerce depend on the cod, but when crops failed, salt fish was the only thing between them and starvation. It was not an easy way for a town to make a living. One venture to the West Indies represented many months of grueling and tedious work: Building the vessel, spending weeks in cold, dangerous waters to catch the cod, drying, salting, and grading the fish, hewing timber into staves, and packing the fish into large barrels.

A sudden North Atlantic storm could swallow the tiny vessel, nullifying all the time and effort. But the people of Salem knew the risks, and in any case, these resilient settlers were well suited to the life. Armed with Bible and Charter, Puritans had a faith as tough as the New England coast, and they believed hard, even menial, labor to be honorable in God's eyes. When Salem Harbor froze over one especially frigid winter, the townspeople spent two weeks chopping a lane in the ice almost a mile long. They took to heart Reverend Peter's admonition, "An hour's idleness is as bad as an hour's drunkenness."

Though the hardships of their lives demanded

"Fish flakes," or drying platforms, were a common feature of colonial fishing ports. Cod were dried here before being packed into barrels for shipment.

people of stern character, and they were undoubt-
edly a sober and diligent lot, they were not the
uniformly grim personalities of the Puritan stereo-
type. Some wore the black, steeple-hatted outfits of
popular tradition, but there were other styles, even
bright colors, as long as the clothing was not "showy"
and women didn't expose "the nakedness of the
arm." When the settlers gained ground in the strug-
gle to survive, they were not above celebrating with
decorous group dancing and singing, although musi-
cal instruments, even a church organ ("the devil's
bagpipes") were banned. Beer, "rumbullion," and
hard cider were universally consumed, but public
drunkenness was strictly outlawed.

The Puritans had found a new home, secure in
God's favor and their growing prosperity. Boston
came to dominate the region's overseas trade, with
Salem a distant but growing second. After decades
of enjoying the commercial benefits of colonial
status, however, Salem's shipowners got a rude
reminder of its drawbacks when they were pulled
into England's feud with France in King William's
War (1689-97). This conflict was the first of the
ongoing French and Indian Wars. Almost until the
Revolution, Salem's commerce was conducted against
a background of sporadic war, with a constant threat
at sea from French privateers.

Vulnerable fishing fleets were a favorite target of
French-Canadian corsairs. After one shot over the
bow, small, unarmed ketches had no choice but to
surrender, so they took to sailing in convoys with
armed escorts. In King William's War, stung by the
blows to their livelihood, Salem merchants outfitted
the armed cruiser *Salem Galley*, which, in a single
day, captured two large French ships off the Cana-
dian coast. Despite these efforts, Salem's fleet was
reduced from 60 vessels to 15 by 1693.

There was danger on land as well. Though France's
Indian allies never attacked Salem directly, they
struck uncomfortably close a number of times. Some
Indians were adept at seizing fishing vessels in port
(never in Salem) and turning them into privateers.

While Salem was trying to cope with the French
and Indians, its troubles were compounded by the
infamous witch trials of 1692. The New England
clergy, having lost ecclesiastical control of suffrage,
were anxious to reassert authority and rekindle

religious fervor. They were given the opportunity when a group of young girls from Salem Village, now Danvers, began accusing people of practicing witchcraft. Fear, revenge, and collective hysteria fed on the town until 200 people were accused, 19 hanged, and one old man pressed to death beneath stones for refusing to plead. Even Philip English, Salem's most prosperous merchant, and his wife were "cried out against." His business was ruined and they were imprisoned, but their money and connections bought them escape to New York until it was safe to return.

As passions subsided the following year, so did the prestige of the clergy and magistrates who had prosecuted so vigorously. These august figures no longer appeared infallible, and in the incipient democracy of the meeting house, Salem's merchants, already the town's richest citizens and for the most part untainted by the tragedy, emerged as political and social leaders.

Two-masted schooners were favored vessels for colonial fishing and the coasting trade.

With the end of King William's War, New England trade quickened and the fisheries were restored. But the new order had to deal almost immediately with a new problem. Since 1663, the colonies had been ignoring the inconvenient provisions of the Acts of Trade requiring that "enumerated articles" be exported only to England or English colonies. American merchants depended on their clandestine trade with French and Spanish ports, and Salem citizens regarded smuggling as respectable. In 1696, however, Parliament began holding colonial governors accountable for breaches of the act, and evasion now demanded more courage and ingenuity. In Queen Anne's War (1702-1713), a Salem captain trading in a French port placed his ship in double jeopardy, risking capture by both French and English privateers.

As the multiplying trade acts put the colonies at a disadvantage, some merchants and captains went beyond smuggling, buying goods from pirates or actually engaging in piracy themselves. The line between officially sanctioned privateering and piracy was vague, and adventurous captains sometimes crossed it, preying on vessels of nations other than those with which England was at war. Some colonies even sent out privateers to extort fishing duties from the vessels of other colonies.

When the common threat of France was past, the old commercial rivalry between Boston and Salem

Benjamin Pickman (1706-73) was one of the early genera-tion of "codfish aristocrats," whose fortunes were built on fishing and foreign trade. He was popular and extremely influential as colonel of the First Essex Regiment and a representative to the Massa-chusetts legislature.

heated up, with Salem slowly cutting into Boston's dominance. But both ports felt the long arm of em-pire when they persisted in buying cheap molasses and sugar from non-British suppliers in the West Indies. Parliament's answer to the British planters' complaints was the 1733 Molasses Act, which im-posed a heavy duty on sugar or molasses imported from foreign islands. Salem urged the General Court (the Massachusetts legislature) to protest the "great decay and the grievous burthen on the West India trade . . . ," but the merchants had to submit. The act dampened the trade, though many honored it only in the breach, continuing to smuggle and bribe customs officials.

The 1730s were a pivotal decade for Salem. Be-fore the 1733 act, the early generations of Salem merchants had enjoyed almost unfettered commerce with the West Indies. That year also brought the death of Philip English, the most prominent merchant of those freewheeling days. Three years later Rich-ard Derby, grandson of Roger Derby, first appeared as a 24-year-old captain for Timothy Orne, Jr. Derby would later take the lead in the fight against Eng-land's increasing determination to restrict colonial commerce, but for now, English's commercial heirs had economic and political control of Salem.

By mid-century, "codfish aristocrats" like Orne and Benjamin Pickman had greatly refined the coastal, West Indies, and overseas trades. Cod was still the staple export cargo and base of the town's economy, but some merchants, led by Orne, were diversifying, working out new trade strategies. American vessels began taking over the Atlantic trade that had been carried in British bottoms. Smaller schooners often played two roles, fishing in the summer, then heading for the West Indies in the fall after the hurricane season and returning in the spring with cargoes for the trans-Atlantic vessels. Expanding the business he inherited from his father, Orne owned seven or eight vessels and bought interests in dozens of voyages. He was probably the most successful merchant in town, having amassed more than £22,000 by the time of his death in 1767.

Native-born sons, grandsons, and great-grandsons of the first generation of merchants were relent-less in building the family businesses. Parliament described them as "merchants [who] keep their ships in constant employ . . . trye[ing] all ports to force a trade. . . . " As leaders, they were also expected to protect the port's interests, so when France again interfered in New England's coastal fisheries, Benjamin Pickman, who was atop Salem's fishing industry, helped organize and finance the successful 1745 campaign against the fortress of Louisbourg in New France. The citizens recognized Pickman's contributions by electing him colonel of the First Essex Regiment, selectman, justice of the Court of Common Pleas, representative to the General Court, and member of the Governor's Council.

Pickman and Orne were the two pillars of colonial merchant society, a small, tight group of about 30 shipowners and their wives. The merchants attended an annual round of parties, teas, and pig roasts, with Pickman occasionally importing live turtles from the West Indies to provide soup for their "turtle frolics." Pickman seems to have been especially popular among his fellow merchants, and he impressed John Adams as "sprightly, sensible, and entertaining."

Young Adams was a frequent visitor to Salem, as were such other Boston luminaries as shipowner and future patriot leader John Hancock and attorney James Otis. While there was some social mixing between the merchants and the professional class of doctors, lawyers, and clergy, they usually moved in different circles. Both groups, however, were in many ways still very British. Upon the coronation of King George II, a group repaired to a tavern and happily "proclaimed" the new king well into the night.

Reflecting the Puritan roots of the town, the merchants continued the old tradition of benevolence by building bridges and roads, funding schools, and helping seamen down on their luck. Timothy Orne once reduced the amount owed him by a woman "because she is a poor widow. . . . " Philanthropy in Salem was not always altruistic, however. In 1760, Pickman and some 30 other merchants founded "a handsome Library of valuable Books. . . ." While the library certainly enhanced Salem's cultural life, it was restricted by the founders to "the sole use of ourselves, Heirs or assigns."

As the town grew more affluent and secure, the Congregational Church grew more tolerant (finally allowing an organ), while holding its dominant place in Salem's social life. Though the English Puritan

Salem merchants displayed their wealth in grand houses. Philip English, a prominent early seatrader, built his "Great House" on English Street in 1685 **(top).** *The steep roof, clustered chimneys, overhanging second story, and casement windows characterized 17th-century New England architecture. The house stood until 1833.*

Colonel Pickman's gambrel-roofed house, built around 1749, was typical of Salem architecture before the Federal style became dominant. It stood on Essex Street beside East India Marine Hall. Pickman acknowledged his debt to the "sacred cod" by mounting a gilt wooden model of the fish on each step of his staircase. A wooden cod still hangs facing the speaker's desk in the Massachusetts legislature.

makeup of the community was somewhat diluted by mid-century with the influx of French Huguenots, Irish, Scots, Dutch, and Germans, Puritan ideals and values for the most part prevailed. Theater was still banned in the community. Dancing, however, was allowed as long as "good order" was maintained, and was extremely popular in town. Bonfires and parades were also favorite diversions. There were of course the rougher pleasures: At one point a cock fight was held in the Town Hall. The sailors, shipyard workers, and ropewalk workers, when fueled with rum, added the threat of violence to the streets of Salem, whether protesting a trade act or celebrating Election Day.

By mid-century, the merchant class had taken Salem from a provincial fishing village to a thriving market town of 5,000. The port had changed much since its Puritan days. The First Church was still a plain building, but it now had a spire looming over the town. Town House Square (now Washington Street) was the civic center of town, the site of Court House, Meeting House, school, and whipping post. On Training Day, livestock shared the common, often called the "Town Swamp," with drilling militia.

After 1700, the town had begun to lose its old-world look as the steep-roofed, casement-windowed dwellings gave way to Georgian-style, gambrel-roofed houses. Richard Derby and a few other merchants still lived on Derby Street near their wharves and warehouses, but Essex Street was the increasingly fashionable site for large, richly furnished houses that John Adams called "the most elegant and grand I have seen in any of our maritime towns." Even in this part of town, though, streets were still unpaved, and during spring thaw, they became a morass that swallowed carriage wheels. In times like these, Mrs. Pickman and Mrs. Orne went shopping in sedan chairs carried by slaves.

The structures supporting their husbands' commerce dominated parts of town. Large sections of the shoreline were covered by hundreds of flakes for drying fish. To cut the costs of processing molasses and hides, merchants built their own distilleries and tanneries, the latter relegated to the area between the Common and Collins Cove because of the smell. For lack of room anywhere else in town, the longest ropewalks were built on pilings over the cove. At Becket's shipyard and those at Knocker's Hole, car-

Richard Derby (1712-83) began as a captain for the codfish aristocracy, but he bought his own fleet and led the new class of aggressive patriot merchants to the top of Salem society. His vessels, commanded by his son John, carried the patriot account of the fighting at Lexington and Concord to England and brought back the first news of the Treaty of Paris. His son Elias Hasket Derby became the preeminent merchant of Salem after the Revolution.

penters turned out more sloops, schooners, and brigs to serve the port's growing commerce.

Commercial traffic in the harbor ranged from trans-Atlantic three-masted ships to schooners from Maine bringing in firewood and timber for the shipbuilders. More wharves held the mounting goods: hogsheads of molasses, casks of rum, sacks of indigo, pipes of wine, stacks of lumber, bundles of hides, and barrels of sugar, salt, fish, and beef. The most important of the new wharves was Union Wharf (now Pickering Wharf), which reached out to and enclosed Jeggles Island in the mouth of the South River. Here, rising merchants like the Derbys and Crowninshields berthed their vessels. Most vessels, though, still worked up to the congested old Wharf Street area at the bend of the South River, where the established merchants owned wharves.

These two groups—the established and the up-and-coming—seemingly differed only in the size of their operations, but deeper differences were brought to the surface when the quarrel with France was renewed in the French and Indian War (1754-63). They both continued to trade in the West Indies despite the dangers from British warships and French corsairs, which captured 23 Salem vessels in less than 16 months. Perhaps because of the extent of the French depredations, however, the older codfish aristocrats were generally more reluctant to deal with French ports, or at least less willing to protest when caught. Their loyalty to Great Britain, despite their breaches of the trade laws, was unquestioned. Some, like Pickman, held royal appointments as magistrates. Others were linked by marriage to British officials in the colonies. With roots going back to the earliest 17th-century colonists, many continued to call England "home."

Neither their scruples nor sentiments were shared by the group of aggressive sea captains like Derby and George Crowninshield, who had learned their trade commanding the vessels of the established merchants. They were buying their own vessels and making inroads on the expanding trade previously monopolized by their employers. More pragmatic and less bound to the mother country, they took advantage of the war to supply both the British and French with war materials. Although they regarded what they did as aggressive business tactics, the British considered it smuggling to the enemy. The merchants were appalled when James Cockle, the newly appointed collector of customs, began seizing vessels that broke acts of trade. A group of Salem and Boston merchants hired lawyer James Otis to protest Cockle's decision to renew licenses to search vessels for smuggled goods. Future President John Adams, present at the trial, later wrote, "American Independence was then and there born. . . ."

The seizures began to seem indiscriminate and unfair to the merchants. Richard Derby, who by this time had retired from the sea to send out his own vessels, was incensed when his schooner *Mary,* sailing under a flag of truce, was seized as a smuggler. Such actions, according to Derby, "set the country on fire." After the French were finally defeated in America, Derby and others still rankled at the memory of the British seizures and fines.

With the end of war, Salem's 53 fishing vessels and 35 trading vessels returned to peacetime trade. In 1763, however, Parliament put teeth into the old 1733 Molasses Act, and the next year passed the Sugar Act, enforcing duties on non-British sugar. These hated laws gave a virtual monopoly of the sugar supply to the British West Indies and cut deeply into Salem's trade. Established families like the Pickmans and Ornes, who had reacted so vigorously to the French presence in Canada, remained passive and conciliatory in the face of Britain's unpopular policies. Their class had lived, indeed thrived, under the old trade acts for a hundred years. Ever the flexible entrepreneurs, they quietly continued to smuggle sugar and molasses from the French West Indies using counterfeit clearance papers.

The rising generation of merchants also continued the clandestine trade, but they had little patience with a distant government that was slowing their climb to prosperity. They resented being made a prime source of revenue for the Crown, and were outspoken, especially Derby and his sons, in their defiance of Parliament and the Salem establishment. This confrontation amounted to more than a temporary class squabble. Its outcome was crucial to the dramatic turn in Salem's commercial fortunes over the next two decades.

Parliament again threatened to claim a piece of the prosperity with the passage in 1765 of the Stamp

A City Facing the Sea

In a city that regularly sent over a tenth of its citizens on dangerous sea voyages, it is understandable that there seemed to be a church steeple in town for every mast in Salem Harbor. The broad spectrum of religious belief in Salem bespoke a diverse society that grew from regular contact with other cities and other peoples. Though small by today's standards, Salem, with 8,000 people in 1790, was the nation's sixth largest city and the richest per capita in that year. Virtually

Derby Wharf, 1797.

surrounded by water, Salem's appearance reflected its dependence on the sea. The waterfront was dominated by sprawling shipyards and the dozens of wharves that extended the city into Salem Harbor. Shipping-related businesses crowded Derby Street and the wharves: warehouses, shops, spar makers, carvers, sail lofts, ship's chandlers, anchor and chain forges, the seaman's church, or "bethel," navigation schools, and instrument makers. Ropewalks took up so much space they had to be built on pilings over Collins Cove near Salem Common.

Merchants conducted business at their waterfront counting houses, although many deals were no doubt struck over an ale at Goodhue's Tavern off Essex Street. This east-west avenue was where the "ancient and respectable families" lived in grand Federal-style houses. The less affluent seamen and artisans lived on the lower ground near the waterfront. On the crowded wharves, high and low mingled with foreign seamen and even an occasional visitor from the East. Salem was both a self-contained community of seafarers and a sophisticated center of world trade.

Detail from painting of Crowninshield (India) Wharf, 1806, by George Ropes, Jr.

Salem in 1805

3 West India Goods Store
To eliminate the middleman
in the local distribution of the
goods he imported, Capt.
Henry Prince built a store
literally in his front yard.

4 Prince House In 1796,
Capt. Henry Prince bought
the house that had been built
in 1762 for Elias Hasket
Derby, Salem's most prominent merchant. The house is
today known as the Derby
House.

5 The Common Called the
"Town Swamp" in its early

8 First Church Erected in
1718, First Church was the
third house of worship for the
Congregational Society, the
oldest Protestant group in
America.

9 Court House A brick
Federal-style building was
built in 1785 to replace the
old court house that had long
stood at the other end of
Washington Street.

10 Pickman House
Benjamin Pickman, an
18th-century merchant, built
his house on Court (later

Salem was one of dozens of
seaports along the New England seacoast in the late 18th
and early 19th centuries.
They ranged from tiny for-
gotten fishing villages to the
great shipping center of
Boston. Some were identified
with a specialized maritime
industry: Nantucket and New
Bedford were whaling ports.
Plymouth, Gloucester, and
Marblehead were successful
fishing ports. Newburyport
was a shipbuilding center.
In its prime, Salem was a
leader in the Far Eastern
luxuries trade. *Map of Salem
Harbor is from 1806 chart by
Nathaniel Bowditch. Map on
facing page shows Salem as it
was in 1805.*

1 Becket's Shipyard
Founded in the mid-17th
century, this was one of the
earliest yards in Salem. Some
of Salem's most famous
vessels were built here.

2 Turner House
Capt. John
Turner grew prosperous in the
17th-century Barbados trade.
He built a large house on
Turner Street near his wharf,
later known as the House of
the Seven Gables.

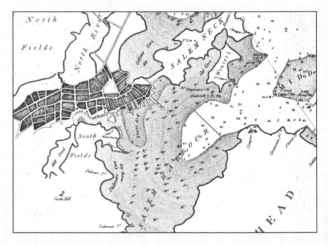

days, the Common was used
for grazing cattle and for
drilling the local militia.
It was later drained, landscaped, and renamed Wash-
ington Square.

6 Briggs' Shipyard This
shipyard on Stage Point,
across from Derby Wharf,
was the most famous in Salem.

7 Derby Mansion For the
16 years that it stood, Derby
Mansion was the grandest
house in Salem. It occupied
an entire block between
Essex Street and Front Street.

Washington) Street, the political center of town.

11 Assembly House Twenty
prominent citizens built
this hall in 1782 for their
social events.

Note: *Some of the buildings
marked on the map no longer
stand, and some have been
moved. The Custom House,
East India Marine Hall
(Peabody Museum), and
Essex Institute were built
after 1805.*

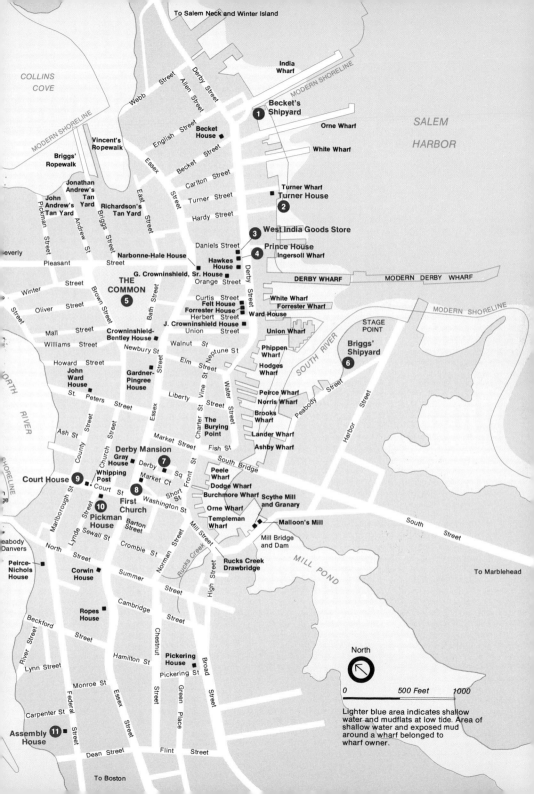

To Salem Neck and Winter Island

COLLINS COVE

MODERN SHORELINE

SALEM HARBOR

India Wharf

1 Becket's Shipyard

Orne Wharf

White Wharf

Webb Street

Derby Street

Allen Street

Becket House

English Street

Essex Street

Becket Street

Carlton Street

Turner Street

Hardy Street

Turner Wharf

2 Turner House

3 West India Goods Store

4 Prince House
Ingersoll Wharf

Daniels Street

Narbonne-Hale House

Hawkes House

G. Crowninshield, Sr. House

Orange Street

Derby Street

DERBY WHARF

MODERN DERBY WHARF

White Wharf

Forrester Wharf

Ward House

MODERN SHORELINE

Vincent's Ropewalk

Briggs' Ropewalk

Jonathan Andrew's Tan Yard

John Andrew's Tan Yard

Richardson's Tan Yard

East Street

Briggs Street

Andrew St.

Pickman Street

Beverly

Pleasant Street

THE COMMON

5

Winter Street

Oliver Street

Mall Street

Williams Street

Brown Street

Bath Street

Curtis Street

Felt House

Forrester House

Herbert Street

J. Crowninshield House

Union Street

Union Wharf

Phippen Wharf

Hodges Wharf

STAGE POINT

6 Briggs' Shipyard

SOUTH RIVER

Crowninshield-Bentley House

Newbury St.

Walnut St

Neptune St.

Elm Street

Vine Street

Water Street

Liberty Street

Charter St.

Peirce Wharf

Norris Wharf

Brooks Wharf

Lander Wharf

Ashby Wharf

Peabody Street

Harbor Street

Howard Street

John Ward House

Gardner-Pingree House

St. Peters Street

Essex Street

Ash St.

Market Street

County Street

Church Street

Derby Sq.

Market Ct.

Front St.

Fish St.

The Burying Point

NORTH RIVER

SHORELINE

Derby Mansion

Gray House

7

Peele Wharf

Dodge Wharf

Burchmore Wharf

Orne Wharf

Templeman Wharf

Scythe Mill and Granary

Malloon's Mill

Mill Bridge and Dam

South Bridge

South Street

To Marblehead

Court House **9**

Whipping Post

8

First Church

10 Pickman House

Marlborough Street

Lynde St.

Sewall St.

Court St.

Washington St.

Short St.

Barton Street

Crombie St.

Norman Street

Mill Street

High Street

Rucks Creek

Rucks Creek Drawbridge

MILL POND

Peabody Danvers

Peirce-Nichols House

North Street

Corwin House

Summer Street

Cambridge Street

Chestnut Street

Ropes House

Beckford Street

River Street

Lynn Street

Hamilton Street

Monroe St.

Carpenter St.

Federal Street

11 Assembly House

Pickering House

Pickering St.

Green Place

Broad Street

Essex Street

Dean Street

Flint Street

To Boston

North

0   500 Feet   1000

Lighter blue area indicates shallow water and mudflats at low tide. Area of shallow water and exposed mud around a wharf belonged to wharf owner.

Pages 34-35: *Salem's wharves were a rich and vital scene, especially when an East Indiaman like the ship* John **(foreground)** *arrived from around the Cape. There was the incessant noise: shouted orders, creaking windlasses, prostitutes beckoning from windows, and sawing and pounding from nearby shipyards. The smells of cinnamon, pepper, cloves, coffee, and tea pervaded the air. In this scene, John, with its long boat and stern boat* **1**, *lies on the harbor mud exposed at low tide around Derby Wharf* **2**. *Crew members off-load sugar from Isle de France* **3** *and cotton from India* **4**. *Dunnage stacked by the bow of the* John **5** *was packed around the cargo to protect it and prevent shifting. Unloaded cargo is being weighed on the customs scale* **6** *and the merchant's tripod scale* **7**. *A coasting schooner at far left has its hull coppered* **8**. *Behind Derby's counting house* **9**, *a lumber schooner* **10** *brings a load of timber to the Hawkes-Babbidge shipyard* **11**. *The ship* Monk **12** *is docked in front of the home of Capt. Samuel Ingersoll* **13**, *now known as the House of the Seven Gables. A fishing boat* **14** *heads out past Orne's wharf* **15**, *where the ex-privateer* Rhodes **16** *is tied up. India Wharf, or Crowninshield Wharf* **17**, *was completed in 1802 by George Crowninshield. A number of Crowninshield's and other merchants' vessels are at India Wharf, including* Belisarius **18**. *At the end of the wharf a stagecoach* **19** *awaits a shore party from a visiting frigate. Beyond India Wharf at far left is Becket's Shipyard* **20**, *where the ship* Fame *was launched in 1802.*

Act, requiring a duty on printed items. The conservative merchants formally protested that the act would be "injurious to liberty, since we are therein tax'd without our consent, having no Representative in Parliament." They would have preferred to let it go at that, but the radical Sons of Liberty, of which Richard Derby, Jr., was a member, seized stamped ship's papers from the Custom House. A large company collected at the London Coffee House, where the papers were denounced and toasts were drunk to King George III and the "Destruction of the Stamp Act."

After a boycott by Boston and Salem of British goods, the Stamp Act was repealed, but Parliament outraged the merchants yet again in 1767 with the enactment of the Townshend Act, which levied duties on paper, glass, painters' colors, lead, and tea. This act laid bare the irrevocable split between the two groups of Salem merchants and pointed up the differences between loyalist-controlled Salem and the more radical Boston. Boston voted to abstain from buying the articles, but Salem's leaders refused to follow suit, prompting an irate letter in the *Boston Evening Post*:

The late management of the town of Salem with regard to this affair is both surprizing and extraordinary. . . . let it be remembered that when we were alarmed at the approach of the Stamp Act these two towns [Salem and Marblehead] *manifested the greatest inclination to comply with it of any towns in the province.*

Salem's elite had set the pace in the port since the 17th century, but now they were swimming against the tide. The taxes levied on the town were becoming truly burdensome, and for most merchants and townspeople, financial considerations were more compelling than abstract questions of liberty or loyalty to the Crown. Fed up by the seizing of vessels, which they denounced as "peacetime privateering," and inflamed by patriotic sermons, the townspeople took matters into their own hands. Their wrath was felt by a customs officer who informed his superiors of a vessel evading duties. He was stripped, covered head to toe with warm tar and feathers, and draped with "Informer" signs. Someone threw a live goose at him. He was then carted the length of Essex Street before a jeering mob and driven out of town.

The old codfish aristocrats, still protesting through channels, were merely voted out of office. Power passed to the patriot merchants in 1768 when Richard Derby, Jr., and John Pickering, Jr., won seats in the General Court. The Derbys had already brought from Rhode Island the patriot journalist and printer Samuel Hall, who published the *Essex Gazette* and the *Essex Almanac* to advocate the patriot merchants' position.

By year's end, British troops were quartered in Boston and men-of-war were stationed off the coast. The prospects for avoiding open conflict grew dimmer. The response of King and Parliament to the 1773 Boston Tea Party was passage of the Coercive Acts, one of which, the Boston Port Act, closed the port and moved its customs officials to Salem. Though the new order in Salem offered more resistance to General Thomas Gage than had the old guard, they displayed a curious blend of political solidarity and commercial opportunism. Salem's leaders petitioned other colonies to cease all trade with British ports until the act was repealed. Despite their call to honor, some Salem merchants continued to handle shipping that normally went to Boston. That port's beleaguered merchants were again angered at Salem's conservative brand of patriotism. Gage's decision to move the seat of government to Salem did not help, especially when the loyalists in town honored him with a parade and ball.

Not wanting to alienate their ideological brothers, Salem's patriot merchants published an open letter to Gage in which they protested:

By shutting up the port of Boston some imagine that the course of trade might be turned hither, and to our own benefit . . . we must be dead to every idea of justice — lost to all feelings of humanity — could we indulge one thought to seize on wealth, and raise our fortunes on the ruin of our suffering neighbors.

In any case, the General Court meeting in Salem refused to cooperate with Gage, supporting Boston and calling for a Continental Congress. After the town staged its own tea party by dumping tea in the streets, Gage packed up for Boston. The General Court then met again in Salem and divorced itself from Parliament's authority, resolving to become an independent Massachusetts Provincial Congress.

In early 1775, after a confrontation at North

Bridge in which Salem citizens barred British soldiers from searching the town for arms, anti-British feelings intensified. Any Tory who expressed "imperfect sympathy" with the patriot cause found himself persona non grata. Life grew intolerable for those who had signed controversial letters of support for the governor. They either recanted or left town. Benjamin Pickman, Jr., with other "friends of government," sailed from Boston for England in March. Many others fled to Nantucket, Nova Scotia, and Bermuda just before the April hostilities in Lexington and Concord, when the real persecutions began.

No loyalist, from judge to Jack Tar, was immune. Some were dragged out at night and flogged on the whipping post. A loyalist minister had his church windows broken. During winter, Tories venturing out on the streets endured a hail of snowballs. Live coals were placed against their doors. The most prominent were often placed under house arrest. Four of those who left, including Benjamin Pickman, Jr., and Judge William Browne, were forbidden to return on pain of death by the 1778 Conspiracy Act.

When economic resistance escalated to revolution, patriot seafarers carried the battle to sea. The port took full advantage of the Continental Congress' decision to augment its tiny navy by licensing hundreds of commercial ships as privateers to harass and capture British vessels. Other vessels carried "letters-of-marque," allowing them to take prizes in the course of regular commercial voyages. Privateering, called by John Adams "a short, easy, and infallible method of humbling the British," was crucial to the American effort in the early years of the war, hurting British commerce, tying up British warships that otherwise could have blockaded American ports, and capturing supplies and arms desperately needed by the Continental Army.

It was a relatively easy matter to convert a merchantman to a privateer, and only a few months after the opening shots of the war, Salem's small but heavily armed schooner *Dolphin* captured the port's first prize—the British trading sloop *Success*. Derby and Union wharves became the center of privateering activity in Salem. Fishermen mounted swivel guns on their fishing smacks and went out in "wolf-packs" to dog the heels of British convoys, cutting out lagging merchant vessels twice their size.

Even the large ships, however, were no match for most British warships. The standard British fighting ship, a third-rate ship of the line, carried 64 to 84 guns ranging from 6- to 32-pounders, while *Grand Turk,* larger than most American privateers, carried only 28 9-pounders. A privateer thus rarely challenged a warship, preying instead on poorly-armed merchantmen. A confrontation was often decided by one broadside, or just the threat of one, so privateering resulted in few casualties.

Salem proved adept at this combination of profit and patriotism. Over the course of the Revolution, the port's 158 privateering vessels took 458 British vessels, accounting for more tonnage than any other American seaport. Many of the prize vessels were refitted and sent out to prey on their former owners.

Although Salem was the only significant New England port to escape capture during the Revolution, the war seriously disrupted Salem's trade. Privateering helped the port survive, in good part by providing jobs for hundreds of seamen and fishermen. The risks were greater than in peacetime trading, but so were the potential rewards. If a seized vessel was judged a lawful prize, half of the auction proceeds went to the owner and the other half to the captain and crew, with some seamen selling their shares in advance for money in hand. For many of Salem's most prominent postwar merchants, privateering profits were the foundation of their fortunes.

Lucrative and exhilarating though it may have been, privateering was no substitute for steady trade. Salem's economy was severely weakened by the war. With the signing of the Treaty of Paris in 1783, the patriot merchants faced the task of rebuilding what their loyalist predecessors had established. They proved more than equal to the challenge. As the codfish aristocrats had taken Salem from a fishing settlement to a thriving market town, the new order would take it from a market town to a center of world trade.

The Sea Traders of Salem

Elias Hasket Derby (1739-99), a maritime merchant of vision and boldness, conceived of a venture beyond the Cape

of Good Hope before learning of the New York ship Empress of China's *pioneering voyage to Canton in 1785. In less than a year he sent* Grand Turk *to Isle de France, from where she sailed to Canton. The risk paid off. He almost tripled his investment on a voyage that made Salem's trade truly global. "Many gathered around him, many imitated his enterprises, & many shared in their success," said Rev. William Bentley in his eulogy to Derby. "The Town was enriched & has become an example to the world."*

"Fortune favors the bold." The ancient maxim is a fitting epitaph for Salem's most successful merchants. Those, like Elias Hasket Derby, to whom the world's riches always seemed to flow were the ones who took chances, dispatching vessels to unproven markets, buying exotic goods, trying the uncharted routes. As went the fortunes of the merchants, so went those of the port.

Risk drove Salem's economic engine during the years following the Revolution. In those days of haphazard insurance, uncertain communications, and predatory vessels, every venture was a gamble, and he who waited for perfect conditions would never have left the wharf. But sheer audacity was equally profitless. The merchant who lacked the wit to shorten sail in the face of high winds, who sailed blindly into dangerous waters, would quickly sink from sight. History remembers most clearly those who succeeded, and the Salem merchants with stories behind their names were those who knew which risks to take.

The willingness to try the unknown was crucial to Salem's recovery after independence. Its merchants emerged from the Revolution with an altered view of the port's future. The traditional boundaries of trade had been established a century earlier, and, though the port's commerce had expanded throughout that period, its merchants had not ventured from the coastal, West Indies, and trans-Atlantic routes. When the new order of patriot merchants raised the port to its central place in American commerce less than a decade after the war, their achievement went beyond restoring lost trade. Tempering vision with native wit, they opened the world's markets to Salem and turned this small fishing and market town, unfavored with a good natural harbor, into a major competitor in world trade.

How did this remarkable generation of merchants work their transformation? Partly through their role

Rev. William Bentley (1759-1819) was an intellectual force in Salem throughout its most prosperous period. Harvard-educated, he was pastor of East Church from 1783 to 1819, during which time he kept a diary of public events and his own highly opinionated observations. He was a complex man: a political partisan who left biased accounts of his perceived enemies, he was also a progressive theologian and thinker who corresponded with European scholars, led the development of Unitarianism in New England, and made his church headquarters for religious and political liberalism in Salem.

in the Revolution. Undeterred by the risks of privateering, Salem shipowners and their captains set the pace. They ranged farther than before, called at distant ports, handled new trade goods. Many other colonial seaports followed Salem's example, but in fleet size, number of prize vessels and cargoes, and profits, the privateer owners of Salem were unrivaled in the thirteen colonies. After taking big risks and tasting the rich payoffs of privateering, they had little appetite for the modest rewards of the old peacetime trade. But more important than the war itself was its aftermath. For Salem, invention was spurred by necessity. Out of its postwar trials came its most dynamic period of trade.

Though the war threw hundreds out of work and privateering had grown less profitable, the port was ambivalent about the end of hostilities. When Richard Derby's son John arrived from Paris in *Astrea* with news of the armistice, one resident recalled that "there were many persons in Salem dejected by the return of peace." With much of its normal trade lost during the war years, privateering had become the fragile base of Salem's economy. Not only did those directly involved in commerce depend on it, but many citizens bought interests in privateering ventures like shares of stock. When the signing of the Treaty of Paris ended privateering, it had the effect of a market crash. Salem's maritime industries, fleet, and workforce, no longer sustained by privateering, were caught in the general postwar depression.

Some trade continued but, compared to the years before the war, Salem was an idle port. Most of the goods on the wharves had been brought there under foreign flags. The fishing fleet was virtually wiped out. Some 54 merchant vessels had been captured by the British, and many others had been damaged. Those that had laid in drydock for the duration also needed refurbishing. But from the shipyards the reassuring sound of the caulkers' mallets, which for so long had set the rhythm of Salem's commerce, was no longer heard. The great winding machines of the ropewalks lay silent over Collins Cove. For the seamen and workers of Salem, it was a bleak time.

The fortunes of most of the merchants survived the war, so they could weather the depression, but for them, too, independence was a mixed blessing. Trade was a different game now. While American shipowners had shed the hated British trade restrictions, they also gave up the benefits of colonial status. They not only lost their monopoly in the West Indies-to-America trade, but until 1796, Great Britain's West Indies ports were closed to its newest competitor. British orders for American-built vessels ceased. The British navy would no longer protect American shipping from Algerian corsairs and foreign privateers.

Salem's merchants began rebuilding their commercial networks. As they tried to restore the old balance of fishing, shipbuilding, and commerce, they did again what their 17th-century ancestors had done. The fishing fleets headed back to the banks. Coasting schooners sailed from Newfoundland to Georgia, selling local produce and "Yankee notions" for corn, flour, tobacco, and naval stores. Smuggling again became an important part of Salem's trade, especially in the banned British West Indies. Those islands badly needed food and did not ask questions when vessels loaded with American produce put into their harbors "under distress." British authorities were helpless before this complicity, fuming that Yankee captains would "swear through a 9-inch plank" to gain entrance to His Majesty's harbors.

In 1784, the first vessels crossed the Atlantic again, carrying hay, oats, and tobacco to Liverpool. Merchants reestablished ties with London bankers and merchant houses. Salem vessels showed their flags again in Bordeaux, Lisbon, and Cadiz, reaffirming European markets.

With the loss of West Indies sugar as a trade staple, merchants experimented with different cargoes, such as almonds and coal, but with little success. Salem's shipowners soon realized that bolder measures were needed to regain prosperity. Competition was more intense. Their vessels now entered foreign ports under the flag of a new, unproven nation. Salem would have to become a different kind of port, one that engaged in a higher level of trade where the stakes were greater. Its ex-privateers, like Derby's *Grand Turk* and *Astrea,* were proving too large in any case to use economically in the West Indies and coastal trades. The owners of ships like these saw the commercial potential of the exotic Eastern goods taken by the vessels as prizes of war. Salem would go to the "Indies" (the Indian Ocean

*Pages **44-45**: 1835 painting by unknown artist shows Salem merchant house flags and pennants of individual vessels.*

In Walden, *Thoreau de-scribed the ideal merchant:*

"If your trade is with the Celestial Empire, then some small counting-house on the coast, in some Salem harbor, will be fixture enough. You will . . . keep up a steady dispatch of commodities, for the supply of such a distant and exorbitant market . . . keep yourself informed of the state of the markets, prospects of war and peace everywhere, and anticipate the tendencies of trade and civilization – taking advantage of the results of all exploring expeditions, using new passages and all improvements in navigation . . . It is a labor to task the faculties of a man – such problems of profit and loss, of interest, of tare and tret, and gauging of all kinds in it, as demand a universal knowledge."

markets) and challenge the old monopolies carved out by the British and European East India Companies almost two centuries earlier. Although the West Indies trade was again a mainstay by 1790, large houses like those of Derby and Crowninshield concentrated on the East Indies and Baltic trades, where the greatest profits lay. The aggressive moves into new markets revitalized New England shipping, pulled Salem out of its depression, and opened the way to prosperity.

One port after another was opened to American trade by Salem vessels. Many of these ships belonged to Elias Hasket Derby, son of Richard Derby and head of the most prosperous house in Salem—the only one to emerge from the war considerably richer. Derby's privateers captured 144 prizes for a profit of almost $1 million. As the nation's greatest privateer owner, head of a leading patriot family, and the wealthiest man in town, other merchants naturally looked to him to lead the way in opening the Eastern trade.

There would be Salem merchants who owned more ships, who made more money than Derby, but none who equaled his impact on the community. He assumed the position previously occupied by men like Pickman and Orne, that of community leader in commerce, government, and social activity. So great was his influence that the (sometimes derogatory) title of "King Derby" fell to this newest merchant prince of Salem. A contemporary described Derby as "a tall man, of fine figure and elegant carriage. His deportment was grave and dignified, his habits regular and exact." His eyes were striking: one blue and one brown. He used no tobacco, and took only an occasional drink.

The most successful of Salem's shipowners had a somewhat unusual career for a merchant. He learned the business from the counting house rather than the quarterdeck. He entered his father's business at 15 and remained there, keeping a watchful eye on the account books and studying naval architecture. He proved so adept at commerce that by 1772, when he was 33, he effectively controlled the business. But he was not driven only by profit. He was a committed patriot (some said "radical"), a member of the Salem Committee of Correspondence who marched with the militia under Timothy Pickering to cut off the British retreat from Lexington. (They arrived too late.) After his father's death in the last year of the war, when Elias was 44, he took the helm of Salem's most powerful merchant house, comprising wharf, warehouses, stores, a distillery, two ships, and three brigs.

Refitting his ex-privateers as large, fast merchantmen, he made bold and imaginative moves to broaden the scope of his trade. In the years following the war, Derby was the first Salem merchant to venture to St. Petersburg, the Cape of Good Hope, Calcutta, Bombay, Madras, Manila, and Canton. From 1775-1800, the Derby house owned nearly a fourth of all the shipping tonnage in Salem. In the last decade of the century, almost a third of the Salem ships to round the Cape of Good Hope were Derby vessels. He was probably America's first millionaire. The Rev. William Bentley, pastor of East Church and chronicler of Salem, wrote, perhaps with some ambivalence, "Wealth with full tide flows in on that man."

Derby's success generated envy. Some disliked his grand style of living, mostly promoted by his wife. A few even attributed his success to "Derby's luck." He was in fact very lucky. He lost only one ship at sea during his entire career. Time after time he found markets for his goods at exactly the right moment. But he created much of his "luck" through close attention to details of ship fitting and safety and a profound knowledge of men. He was respected by the majority of people in Salem, who readily acknowledged his preeminence.

He was the one who took the early chances, often with only 50-percent insurance, experimenting with new markets that sometimes, like his venture to the Barbary Coast, failed. He was an innovator, the first Salem merchant to use a supercargo, or seagoing business agent, on a voyage, and one of the first American merchants to sail vessels with coppered bottoms. He developed a centralized world trade network and a system for consigning his cargoes to a foreign house, which relieved his supercargoes of the need to deal with a long succession of buyers.

His influence lived in the next generation of prominent captains and merchants. "Derby's Boys," many of whom began their careers in his counting house before going to sea on his training vessels, were legion: his sons John and Elias Hasket, Jr.,

Capt. George Crowninshield (1734-1815) was the tough and aggressive patriarch of the seafaring clan that contributed so many captains and merchants to Salem.

The Rise of the Crowninshields

At the zenith of their power, George Crowninshield and Sons was one of the leading shipowning families in New England. The Crowninshield fleet comprised 16 vessels in 1809—the second largest in Salem. The business was managed in Salem by George, Sr., George, Jr., and Benjamin, who also sat in the state legislature. Jacob was in Washington as Chairman of the House Committee on Commerce and Manufactures. Richard was the family agent in New York,

and John served the same function in Bordeaux. Their rise to the top had been rapid, and their aggressive, litigious style had not endeared them to the Salem aristocracy, especially the Derbys. George, Sr., who had been a captain for Richard Derby before the Revolution, was characterized as a "bluff, warm-hearted chivalrous seaman" and "a son of nature [with powers] such as are employed only in seafaring." Even after George and Derby's son Elias Hasket had

Detail from painting of Crowninshield Wharf, 1806, by George Ropes, Jr.

*The Crowninshield brothers, George, Jr. (1766-1817) **1**, Jacob (1770-1808) **2**, and Benjamin (1772-1851) **4**, and their aunt Elizabeth Crowninshield (1735-99) **3**, who married Elias Hasket Derby.*

married each other's sister and George began to acquire ships of his own after independence, the Crowninshields remained unpopular, labeled as "Base Plebians" and "Sons of Pride." The five sons continued to serve Derby and other merchants as captains, especially in the East Indies trade. Each had studied navigation at 12, gone to sea at 15, and commanded a vessel by age 20. Jacob was handsome, charming, articulate, and a congressman at 32. Ben, more stolid and businesslike, was the real director of the firm, with other careers as bank president, Secretary of the Navy, and congressman. The family continued to prosper and acquire ships, and by 1800 the poor relations of the Derbys had become one of their chief competitors. In the next decade they led a quiet revolution in Salem—supplanting the older Federalist merchant aristocracy with the newly-affluent Republican upstarts. They established the Merchants Bank, became philanthropists, and published a newspaper to counter the Federalist *Salem Gazette.* Riding the Jeffersonian tide, they became the new order in Salem.

Salem. N° 3.

These are to Certify that Samuel Webb was by a Majority of Votes regularly admitted a Member of the Salem Marine Society, at a Meeting held the 25 day of March 1795 Given under my hand & the Seal of the Society this 6 day of Nov. A.D. 1797.

Jos.ᵃ Mansᵗᵉʳ Sec.ʸ
Benj.ⁿ West   Master

Joseph Peabody, Nathaniel Bowditch, four Crowninshield brothers, Nathaniel Silsbee, Stephen Phillips, Richard Cleveland, Ichabod and Jacob Nichols, Henry Prince, Benjamin and Ebenezer West, his nephews John and Thomas Prince, and his sons-in-law Nathaniel West and Benjamin Pickman, Jr.

Derby was demanding of employees, but he evoked great loyalty from his captains and respect from Salem shipbuilders for his "intuitive faculty in judging of models and proportions." Unlike some merchants, he was considerate of his crews, making sure that his vessels were stocked with fresh vegetables. If one of his crew members died, Derby provided for the family.

With business associates he was forceful—some would have said opportunistic and inflexible. Even his admirer Reverend Bentley called his behavior on one occasion "detestable." But despite his hard-edged entrepreneurship, he was known to be strictly fair in his business dealings. To his everlasting credit, he set a good example for other merchants by forbidding his captains to carry slaves on his vessels.

Though this stern figure might not have been universally loved in the business world, he seems to have been good company away from work, described by one acquaintance as "affable, mild, and cheerful." He shared his wealth, often making his charitable bequests in secret.

The merchant society that Derby headed was a small, self-enclosed group. A few names remained prominent through the years: Prince, Hodges, Nichols, Peirce, Silsbee, Crowninshield, West, Ropes. While they were a different group of families from those who made up the codfish aristocracy, the break was not complete. Loyalist Benjamin Pickman, Jr., returned after the Revolution, was "reclaimed," and made the Pickman name respected again. William Orne, whose family had been one of the most important in pre-war commerce, was an early venturer in the Baltic and Canton trades.

Although some sons of the more prosperous merchants attended Harvard before joining the firm, a practical education was more typical, with the young man coming back to the counting house by way of the quarterdeck. After attending school until age 14, he put in his time at the clerk's bench, where he learned debits and credits. In Derby's counting house he also learned navigation from retired captains. After two or three years he shipped out on a vessel as a captain's clerk or "writer," tending books for the captain and supercargo. An adventurous few shipped out as common seamen, but the typical merchant family scion avoided the rough forecastle life. He escaped the dirtier and more dangerous jobs of the seaman, but was expected to stand watches and learn the basics of a sailing vessel.

Next he sailed on a small vessel as supercargo. If he performed his duties well, showed leadership, and mastered navigation, he would be given command of a small vessel in the coasting or West Indies trade. Derby's training ship *Rose* regularly sailed to the West Indies under command of a first-time captain. Gradually receiving commands on larger vessels, the young captain sailed the trade routes, learning the sea and the ways of foreign traders. As he accumulated capital from his private "adventures," he bought interest in the vessels he sailed, eventually retiring from the quarterdeck to work for his family or send out his own vessels.

To succeed in the highly competitive atmosphere of Salem commerce, he needed infinite patience and the temperament to operate in the shifting relationships among the town's merchants, where a partner on today's voyage might be a competitor on tomorrow's. Commerce demanded an intimate knowledge of the world's commodities, their constantly changing markets, and the myriad conditions that could alter them, such as weather, economic depression, piracy, and war. A knowledge of men was crucial, as was the right balance of strength and flexibility that would earn their respect and loyalty. Perhaps most important was the willingness to take risks.

These men were speculators, not suppliers. They embodied the spirit of capitalism rooted in early Puritan trade. They accepted risk and ruin as part of their lot, and fortunes rose and fell precipitously. After staking everything on one voyage, Richard Cleveland returned to Salem penniless. George Nichols wrote in his memoirs, "Then came a long series of disasters, ruinous voyages . . . bad management . . . I found myself bankrupt . . . reduced in a few years from affluence to complete destitution."

Such a group of strong-minded entrepreneurs cannot easily be characterized. Contrasted to William Gray's pious sobriety was the volatile Simon Forrester, the boisterous ex-seaman described by Bentley as a "ship without a helm." (He was disciplined enough, however, to leave an estate of more than one million dollars.) Jacob Crowninshield was suave and elegant, while it was said of William Orne that, despite his name, rough charm, and liberal hospitality, he was "without culture." Careers ran the gamut from that of Elias Hasket Derby, who rarely, if ever, went to sea, to Richard Cleveland, who stayed at sea for years at a time, buying ships wherever he could and commanding them himself.

It is safe to say, however, that true to the community's Puritan roots, they had an aversion to idleness. In their memoirs and logs they noted condescendingly the "indolence" and "sloth" of the people of distant lands they visited as shipmasters. Careers were accelerated by today's standards, and early advancement was expected. The Salem Marine Society would not admit anyone over 40 without a special vote by the members. It was not unusual for a man barely out of his twenties to be sending vessels around the world, have a large house on Essex Street, and be an influential member of Salem society.

Though they were a very small and distinctly elitist group, the merchants maintained the tradition of community spirit and philanthropy. They spent their money freely in the town, providing work for artisans, tradesmen, and laborers. The grand houses and public buildings they commissioned gave Salem an elegance and sophistication unusual for so small a city. They were, of course, not all lovable, altruistic people. Some put their ventures above all else. When William Orne, one of Salem's greatest philanthropists, heard that pirates had taken one of his vessels and killed the entire crew, including his nephew the captain, he reportedly responded, "At least the vessel was insured."

Although we must assume that most Salem merchants were not such icy souls, it was typical that Orne had a close relative sailing his vessel. Among Salem's merchant class, family ties were all-important, and family and commerce were inextricably bound. Shipowners preferred to hire their captains and supercargoes from among relatives, both to strengthen class solidarity and to reduce the risks of trade. Business partnerships were often among relatives for the

Simon Forrester (1748-1817) came to Salem as an Irish seaman at 19. By 28 he had his own command and was one of Salem's most successful privateer captains, capturing four British ships in 1776. After independence, he turned merchant and shipowner and sent some of the earliest ventures to the profitable Baltic area. He was characterized as headstrong, with a "temper as boisterous as a Tempest," but honorable and generous. At his death he left $1.5 million.

Salem's Master Builder

Successful merchants who wanted to give a face to their prosperity often turned to Samuel McIntire (1757-1811), "the architect of Salem." McIntire early demonstrated his flair for the new Federal style in the house on Federal Street (right) he designed in 1782 for Jerathmiel Peirce. The third floor is gracefully foreshortened, while the fence urns attest to McIntire's skill as a woodcarver. Called the Peirce-Nichols House, it is considered one of the finest houses of the early

Federal period. McIntire's long connection with Elias Hasket Derby began when Derby's wife Elizabeth persuaded him that their position demanded a more imposing house. They bought the old Pickman house on Court (later Washington) Street and in 1786 asked McIntire to completely remodel it (below). Mrs. Derby's still-unsatisfied ambitions led to McIntire's largest project. The Derby mansion and grounds (above) occupied the entire block between

Essex Street and the waterfront where the Old Town Hall now stands. McIntire reworked Charles Bulfinch's original exterior plan and designed a beautiful interior noted for its oval rooms. McIntire's and Bulfinch's

drawings for the house are in the Essex Institute collections. After five years of construction, Derby and his wife moved into the house in 1799, but both died within a few months.

McIntire's massive corner pilasters on Derby's Court Street house and his model for the interior Corinthian capitals (inset) *typified his classical motifs.*

William Gray (1750-1825) was one of the greatest individual shipowners in the United States. He owned interest in 181 vessels in his lifetime and was worth $3 million at the time of the 1807 embargo on foreign trade. For his support of the embargo he was so ostracized by other Salem merchants that he moved to Boston in 1809. During the War of 1812, he outfitted the frigate Constitution *at his own expense. In peacetime, Gray's ships specialized in the Mediterranean-to-Calcutta trade.*

same reason. By pooling capital, a family could send out ventures impossible for an individual merchant.

Marriage alliances between prominent merchant families further strengthened a class highly conscious of its privileged position and increased the pool of trusted employees and partners. Often, two prominent family trees would become intricately connected, with many first- and second-cousin marriages. When Elias Hasket Derby's ship *Benjamin* left the wharf, his nephew Charles was first mate. The captain, Nathaniel Silsbee, married Derby's niece, Mary Crowninshield, whose brothers, Jacob and Benjamin, were also Derby captains. Their father, George Crowninshield, married Derby's sister Mary, and Derby married Crowninshield's sister Elizabeth. Jacob married another of Derby's nieces. Derby's daughter Martha married her cousin John Prince, a captain for Derby's son John, who had also been a captain for his father, as had Elias Hasket, Jr.

When associates could not be drawn from family, merchants formed loose partnerships with friends or political allies. Before banking and insurance companies were formed at the end of the 18th century, merchants commonly financed and underwrote each other's voyages. Only the wealthiest could afford to own vessels outright. Most owned shares: anywhere from half to a thirty-second and smaller. Not everyone who invested in a venture was a merchant, however. Bankers, professionals, and prosperous artisans all bought shares in ventures, much like playing the commodities market today.

Business was often a relatively informal affair. Two merchants might meet on Derby Wharf and agree to split the cost of a cargo of South Carolina rice. Or one would suggest that they step into his counting house, where they planned something larger, such as sending a cargo of rum, cod, and shingles to Cadiz. A truly ambitious undertaking might call for a meeting in the fraternal atmosphere of Sun Tavern (called King's Arms before independence).

It is easy to imagine them sitting around the table, striking a deal over Indian cheroots and spiked punch. The owners of an East Indiaman want to send a cargo of American, West Indian, and European goods to Isle de France and Batavia, with the intent of bringing home pepper, cotton, and ivory. They need investors to help purchase the outward cargo. The prospect of a 100-percent profit entices three to buy shares in the venture. Now the voyage must be insured against the possibility of disaster. Eight say they have enough confidence in the owner, vessel, and captain to take the gamble and underwrite the venture. The deal is made.

At the end of the business day, usually around mid-afternoon, Salem's merchants returned to homes that reflected the general success of these ventures. Around the turn of the century, those with homes on Derby Street began to desert the increasingly rambunctious waterfront for three-storied Federal-style houses up on Essex Street, Chestnut Street, and Washington Square. Most of these houses were built by, or showed the influence of, Salem's arbiter of taste and dominant architect, Samuel McIntire, whose clean lines and restrained elegance reflected the no-nonsense businessmen for whom he built.

The post-Revolutionary merchants, inasmuch as they intermarried and formed a self-conscious group, were like the old codfish aristocrats. Unlike their predecessors, however, most were not from wealthy old families. They were self-made, plainspoken people with limited formal educations who strove to refine themselves. Those who could sent their sons to Harvard. They advertised their status and worldliness through their homes, stocking their shelves with Eastern delicacies and displaying exotic furnishings, especially Canton china and silks. As they amassed capital and acquired land, they reached for genteel status, just as the earliest Salem tradesmen had made themselves into respected merchants.

Despite this upward striving, Salem's postwar merchant society was less formal than the earlier one. Wigs and knee breeches gave way to natural hair with plaited "queues" (pigtails) and trousers made of nankeen and seersucker brought back from the East. The merchants proved uninhibited enough to turn out in full Oriental dress for the opening of East India Marine Hall, and it became the fashion for their wives to dress in silk Oriental gowns at home. Dances were the major social events, where they reeled to fiddle and piano music. Informal afternoon outings included carriage and sleigh rides and fishing parties. The latter featured hot chowder and Madeira wine from prized old bottles with labels like "*Astrea* 1787," showing the year and vessel in which it arrived in Salem.

The wealthiest acquired nearby country estates they called "farms." Most notable of these was Derby's Oak Hill, complete with McIntire carvings and furniture and a herd of "Cape of Good Hope Sheep." An "Alsatian Gardner" tended the experimental crops and gardens.

Behind such trappings of gentility, competition among Salem merchants remained intense. No post-Revolutionary commercial, social, and political rivalry was more notorious than that between the Federalist Derbys and the Republican Crowninshields. Ironically, the families had a great deal in common. George Crowninshield, like Richard Derby, had commanded vessels for Timothy Orne, and then for Derby himself. The Crowninshield brothers followed their father as masters on Derby vessels. There were two Derby and three Crowninshield houses along a two-block stretch of Derby Street. Derby and the elder Crowninshield were even brothers-in-law.

Despite all these ties, the two families moved apart and invariably took opposing sides on political and social issues. The Derbys were a socially prominent family with roots going back to the 17th-century English colonists in Salem. They epitomized the patriot merchants who became conservative Federalists and ruled post-Revolutionary New England. Although Federalists especially mistrusted the French, all foreigners were suspect in Salem. Thus the German Crowninshields, aggressive and litigious, maintained a precarious social position despite their commercial success, and were driven into the Republican fold. Derby and Crowninshield were both proud, fierce partisans who became, in the Reverend Bentley's words, "sworn enemies." In 1796, Derby brought suit against Crowninshield, claiming that the latter's nearby wharf projected too far into the harbor channel, causing Derby's wharf to silt up. After the court forced Crowninshield to shorten his wharf by 12 feet, bad feelings grew worse. So bitter was the animosity that not one Crowninshield attended the 1799 funeral of Elizabeth Crowninshield Derby, George Sr.'s sister and Derby's wife.

After Derby's death the same year, the fortunes of the Derby family declined along with the Federalist party, while those of the Crowninshields rose. The Derby house proved fragile without the strong foundation of its patriarch. Sons John and Elias Hasket, Jr., continued to send vessels to the Mediterranean and the East, but the vision—Derby's "uncommon spirit of enterprise"—was gone. They lost influence, even became an embarrassment, as their prolonged disputes over the estate were waged in public. After Nathaniel West divorced Derby's daughter and claimed the Derby farm, he and his brother-in-law Hasket Derby had a fist fight on Derby Wharf. Family members moved away and the Derby flag disappeared from Salem.

But in Salem there was always a strong merchant or merchant family to fill a vacuum at the top, and after the death of Elias Hasket Derby, William Gray assumed his place. In the early years of the 19th century, he became the greatest individual ship-owner of his time, with over 30 vessels and employing about 300 men annually. "Billy" Gray was a short, rough-hewn man, who was somewhat more easygoing than Derby. He was pious, strong in his convictions, and, important in a Puritan town that disapproved of imperious behavior and overweening pride in its plutocrats, "unostentatious, plain, and affable in his manners."

Perhaps most noteworthy about Salem's merchants was that there generally was no professional barrier between merchants and their captains. Each generation of merchants had commanded vessels belonging to the generation they would succeed. As Richard Derby sailed for Timothy Orne, George Crownin-shield sailed for Richard Derby and Jacob Crownin-shield sailed for his father. Many merchants had only recently braved the Eastern seas, and captains often took financial risks as investors. Some even owned outright the vessels they commanded.

This system ensured that the merchant knew the worth of good crews and was aware of their trials at sea. When he sent out a valuable vessel with a large part of his fortune tied up in its cargo, he knew that the success of the voyage depended on how the captain, supercargo, and crew handled the jobs he had performed in his youth. In turn the citizens of Salem understood that the health of their community depended on the boldness and vision of its shipowners.

Toilers of the Sea: The Crews

Sailors on East Indiamen had the coveted berths on the largest and fastest vessels. The crew of Grand Turk *endured the longest voyage yet by a Salem vessel — six months at sea and halfway around the world. Violent North Atlantic winter storms were followed by a passage through the treacherous Straits of Malacca at Sumatra. Their reward was being the first New England crew to see China.*

"From father to son, for above a hundred years, they followed the sea; a gray-headed shipmaster in each generation retiring from the quarter-deck to the homestead, while a boy of fourteen took the hereditary place before the mast, confronting the salt spray and the gale which had blustered against his sire and grandsire."
— Nathaniel Hawthorne

Salem's prosperity was only as strong as its seamen. Once a vessel left the wharf, the fate of a venture was in the hands of a small community of sailors ranging the world's immense oceans. Salem's commercial success was eloquent testimony to their skills.

At the dedication of East India Marine Hall in 1824, the merchants of Salem drank a toast to "the strong limbs, hard faces, and free-born manners of our Sailors." They knew how important "the people," as they called them, were to their enterprise. A brilliantly conceived and well-equipped venture could prove a dismal failure if the crew were not as good as their vessel. The greenest seaman could endanger a voyage by improperly roving a lanyard through the deadeyes of a shroud. A mast thus poorly secured and carrying full sail could snap like a matchstick in a high wind. A supercargo unable to keep pace with the shrewd traders of the world could ruin his employer. A captain who lacked good instincts or navigational skills could bring the voyage to an abrupt and ignominious end on a shoal thousands of miles from home.

These realities of maritime trade made trust one of Salem's strongest currencies. The Salem community had faith in the captain and seamen, and the crews put their lives in the hands of the shipbuilders and craftsmen. When the anchor cable was the only thing holding their vessel off a reef during a storm, the crew had to believe that the ropewalk workers had done their job well. As they lay in their bunks with the cold North Atlantic inches from their heads, they had to believe that the men who built and sealed the hull knew their business.

Salem's crews were, to use the words of one seaman, "a hetergenious mass of incongruity" — a mix of salty veterans and raw boys who didn't know aft from hawse hole. The majority were from New Hampshire and Massachusetts, especially the coastal towns of Essex County. Nearly all classes were

This day took unboard 9¼ pipes wine and 3 Gang Casks of water which compleats our Cargo of Wine & compliment of water — got the Boats in their Births — swayed up the TG masts and prepared everything for sea — weather moderate & pleasant ————————

13th

At 8 AM a Boat came from shoar and weighed the stream Anchor, we unmoor'd Ship — it being Ebb tide we lay still for the flood — at 1 PM it made to the NE and we began to heave; it started when we had 50 fathoms Cable out. lay the ships head offshoar under easy sail and at ½ past 3 we got the Anchor to the bow being 3 leagues to the Westward of Orabava: at 4 PM I came onboard. discharge the Pilot and stood to the Westward — at 8 PM the W. end of the Island bore SSW distance 4 leagues — a good breeze of ENE: at midnight GOMERO bore SSW 6 leagues distance ————————

14th

From midnight to 4 AM a fresh breeze from NNE which caused us to close reef the T Sails — the morning more moderate when we made sail — at 4 Gomero bore E 3 leagues — employed in unbending Cables stowing Anchors & clearing Ship at Noon the Peak of Tenerife bore ESE and the SW part of Ferro WBN ½ N — our Lat.: was 27.47 N — from now I shall begin my sea JOURNAL —

Prospect of Santa Cruz off Tenerife.

15th

At noon the Peak bore EBN distance 19 leagues; from which I take my departure, its Latitude being 28°.13 N. and Longitude 16.36 W — pleasant weather Ship under all sail — from the appearance of the Sea & difference between the Log and Observation, I suppose we had a strong current to the NE for the first 12 hours between Gomero and Ferro; I allow 1½ point Variation Lat. by Observation 26.13 N

16th

These 24 hours pleasant Gales & clear Weather — Employed in removeing Beef, Butter &c from foreward to aft, for the better trim of the Ship Latitude pr Observation 24.52 North —

                                                                   16th

represented among the seamen. Most were Anglo-Saxon, with a fair number of black Americans and Europeans among them. Surprisingly, fishermen rarely made the transition to merchant vessels. They were an independent breed who refused to spend long periods away from home and scorned set wages, preferring to "fish on their own hook."

Though some seamen were the "adventure-seeking boys" described by historian Samuel Eliot Morison, most probably went to sea for more mundane reasons. To many farm boys, the lure of steady wages outweighed the dangers. For others, obtaining a berth was the only way to reduce the number of hungry mouths in a poor family. There were always a few British deserters and men on the run. A minority were provided berths by friends or relatives who owned or commanded a vessel. When Martha Prince of Nova Scotia sent her son John, with a jar of "rasbery gam" under his arm, to her brother Elias Hasket Derby in Salem, she could be sure that a berth would be found for him.

The shipboard careers of most seamen were relatively brief. They spent a few years at sea and returned to shore life with a nest egg. The outstanding seaman might go on to become captain, and even continue sailing until retirement, but those who made wise investments often retired early to a safer profession. Commercial sailing was thus a young man's calling. The average age of a crew, including captain and officers, was around 22, and apprentice seaman were typically adolescents. The crew of *Benjamin* on her successful voyage to the Indies in 1792 was made up of "Derby's Boys": Capt. Nathaniel Silsbee was only 19. His first mate Charles Derby was 20, and clerk Richard Cleveland, 18. Older seamen in their 30s, 40s, and sometimes 50s made up a small part of the crew, but generally represented the hard-luck cases of forecastle society. This kind of sailor often drifted from port to port and drink to drink until he grew too old to haul on a line and lived out his final days in a sailor's home.

Unlike naval or privateering vessels, commercial ships carried only enough crewmen to handle the rigging. Generally, a vessel needed one man for every 15 tons. But the size of the crew was also determined by the vessel's rig; thus a 250-ton square-rigged ship required more men than a schooner of

Of Capt. Benjamin Carpenter (1751-1823) a contemporary wrote, "He followed the seas the principal part of thirty years with the character of an intelligent, generous, and very active man." He was also instrumental in founding the East India Marine Society, which gathered the original collection of the Peabody Museum. Captain Carpenter's drawings illustrate his log (left) for the 1792 voyage of the ship Hercules to the East Indies. This sketch is of Santa Cruz de Tenerife, in the Canary Islands.

the same capacity. The crew on a small trans-Atlantic schooner might include only a captain, mate, and five seamen, while as many as 20 men would sail on a large East Indiaman.

For weeks at a time, their world was a small vessel on a vast blue reach. Life on board ranged from pleasant to terrifying, depending on wind and water. There were the good days when the ship ran well before a stiff following wind and the work was not too hard. The creaking of the timbers and the rhythmical splash of the bow wave were the comforting sounds of a vessel making good way.

Then there were the dispiriting times when the wind died and the sails hung limply from their yards. The becalmed ship was no longer a sailing vessel; it was a hull adrift. Worst were the Equatorial Doldrums, between the trade wind belts, and the Horse Latitudes, 30° N and S, so named because becalmed vessels threw horses overboard to save water. The sun glanced off unruffled water, and the still air was harsh in the lungs.

But even the worst of the doldrums were preferable to the other extreme. A small vessel was nearly helpless when caught in the forces of a bad North Atlantic storm. As gale-force winds pushed up 45-foot waves, the crew forced themselves up bucking ratlines to take in canvas, as the spars could not long bear the strain of 50-knot winds on full sails. The helmsman, his visibility reduced by flying spray, fought to keep his vessel off the wind so it would not be pushed over. In the hold below, seamen pumped 1,200 strokes an hour to keep it from flooding.

To withstand such extremes of boredom and danger, a crew had to submit to strict routine and a rigid hierarchy presided over by the captain. The first and second mates were experienced seamen with the ability to whip into shape boys fresh off the farm. Below the officers were mariners with specialized skills, such as sailmakers and carpenters. They, like the cook, were called "idlers" because they had no specific role in working the ship. Those who did work the ship were the able-bodied (fully-trained) and ordinary seamen. On the bottom rung were the apprentices, or "greenhands," who performed the hardest, dirtiest, and most dangerous jobs.

Outside the hierarchy was the supercargo, who represented the owners' interests and conducted business negotiations. Salem supercargoes were often Harvard graduates, or had served a term of apprenticeship in a counting house and as captain's clerk to learn the mysteries of profit percentages. Some supercargoes with enough shipboard experience "came in through the cabin window" to become captains.

Salem's most distinguished supercargo, Nathaniel Bowditch, was known world-wide for his contributions to the science of navigation. When he sailed with Capt. Henry Prince on *Astrea* on its voyage to the Philippines in 1796, Prince remarked that there was "more knowledge of navigation on board the *Astrea* than ever there was in all the vessels that have floated in Manila Bay." Bowditch taught lunar reckoning to 12 of the crew members, and for years afterward, a seaman's claim that he had sailed with Bowditch was a ticket to a mate's berth.

Beside their navigation duties, the first and second mates took charge of the two watches, starboard and larboard, into which a ship's company on a large vessel was divided. Each group stood alternate 4-hour watches around the clock, with two 2-hour "dog watches" to ensure that a seaman would not stand the same watches every day. The rhythms of shipboard routine were set by the ship's bell, which struck as the sand glass was "capsized" every half-hour: one bell at 12:30 a.m, two bells at 1:00 a.m., up to 8 bells at 4, when the sequence began again.

When sails were set, seamen were put to the chores that kept a vessel seaworthy: polishing the decks with brick-like holystones, mending sails and rigging, going aloft with buckets of grease and tar to slush the spars and tar down the rigging. It was from performing this last task that sailors earned the name "tars." When everything else was done, the mates could always have them pick oakum—pull apart old rope and rags for caulking material. At the command to put on more sail, some scrambled up the ratlines and out onto the yards to untie the reef points. Others pulled the belaying pins securing the halyards and prepared to haul. Hoisting a yard was made easier by rhythmic work chanteys, with two pulls on each chorus:

A Yankee ship came down the river,
Blow, *boys,* blow.
And all her sails they shone like silver,
Blow, *my bully boys,* blow.

Capt. John Carnes (1755-96) succeeded as captain of both privateer and merchant vessels. After capturing a number of British vessels during the Revolution, he was named commodore of a West Indies privateer fleet in the last year of the war. Following independence, he commanded commercial vessels in the East India trade, as did his brother Jonathan, famous for opening Salem's lucrative Sumatra pepper trade.

Master of the Quarterdeck

With every voyage a captain put his reputation on the line. Sustained success in this profession took a sharp mind and grace under pressure, but Salem's captains had no typical temperament, came from no predictable background. Some were salty men of the sea; others were seagoing businessmen. Some were scions of Salem seafaring families, groomed from child-hood for command. Others were farm boys who had gone to sea and made good. All of them bore tremendous responsibilities. Once a vessel cleared the wharf, it became the captain's domain and he was absolute master. The shipowner entrusted to him his ship, his cargo, the lives of the crew, and the good name of his company. The captain in effect became the company. A trusted captain was allowed much discretion in how he disposed of the cargo. Elias Hasket Derby added this note to his very specific sailing orders to Capt. Samuel Williams: "I do not mean the above as Positive Orders. You hereby have my leave to Proceed in any way different that you by Calculation shall find more for my advantage."

Thus, being able to handle tough seamen, make split-second decisions in a gale, and navigate a ship through poorly-charted waters was not enough. He also had to judge the quality of numerous goods, keep up with world markets and prices, and deal with shrewd foreign merchants. All this from a captain often in his twenties. But by that time he had been to sea five or ten years and learned every rope and port. If he had started as a seaman, he "came up through the hawsehole" to command, typically at 19 or 20. Many, especially the sons of merchant families, had put in a few years in the counting house before going to sea. If the business side of the trade appealed to them, they could serve as captain's clerk and then supercargo (a seagoing business agent and often a college graduate) before coming to command "through the cabin window." Some had part interest in the ships they commanded, and most were allowed up to five tons of cargo for private "adventures." An ambitious captain could retire from the sea by age 30 to send out his own vessels.

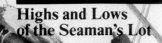

Highs and Lows
of the Seaman's Lot

A sailor could not be claustrophobic or very tall, as his quarters in the forecastle ("focs'le") were cramped, dark, and damp—cold in winter, stifling in summer. Its walls were pounded during storms because it was located close to the bow of the vessel, "before the mast." But the forecastle was home to the sailor at sea, where he tried to sleep between watches and manfully downed his often vermin-infested hardtack, dried peas, and salt meat. Off-duty seamen played cards, made music, and, if ambitious, studied navigation from their "Bowditch."

There were as many reasons for signing on a sailing vessel as there were men. Some needed a living wage. Some were one step ahead of prison or deserters from the British Navy. There were farm boys escaping the drudgery of the plow. All found they had to earn whatever they were looking for at sea. It was a life of hard work, poor food, spartan conditions, and long hours of tedium punctuated by moments of stark terror. A sailor couldn't hesitate when told to climb swaying ratlines during a winter storm to yards 50 or 100 feet above the deck, then inch out on icy footropes and, with numb fingers, gather heavy, frozen sails that could throw him to his death with one violent flap. Hence his creed for survival: "One hand for the ship; one hand for yourself." Of course there were compensations. At 22, he would see cities like Canton and Calcutta, while those he left behind might never see Boston. Capt. Richard Cleveland, who spent years before the mast, recalled that "no profession is so easy, so pleasant, so free from care as the seaman's." Unlike his European brethren, an American seaman could aspire to his own command. But until that time, he had to prove he could "hand, reef, and steer," that is, furl a sail, reef a sail, and stand a trick at the wheel, holding a steady course by a 32-point compass. He had to "know the ropes," be able to lay his hand instantly on the right one, at night, out of dozens coming down out of the dark. Only then could he call himself a seaman.

His Worldly Goods

For a sailor thousands of miles from home, his sea chest was his seat, table, tool box, valuables safe, food locker, and respite from boredom. Many spent off-hours on fancy ropework, shown on the chest handles. Among the typical items in a chest were (counterclockwise) white linen pants and a canvas hat waterproofed with tar; an octant and a "Bow-ditch" on navigation; a Bible; pipes and a twist of tobacco; a whalebone ditty box; a slung shot—a weapon consisting of a lead ball in a knotted pouch; knife and fork; razor and strop; soap dish; splicing fids, pricker, knife, and seamer palm for mending sails; sewing kit; and medicine.

71

Jonathan Haradan (1744-1803), Salem's most successful and famous privateer captain during the Revolution, was celebrated for his resourcefulness, icy calmness under fire, and the absolute loyalty of those under him. He never lost a ship, and was said to have captured more than 60 vessels carrying perhaps 1,000 guns and 2,000 to 3,000 men.

To avoid the mate's boot, an apprentice had to quickly "learn the ropes." He also learned a few rules that would keep him alive: Go aloft on the windward rigging, so you'll be pushed against it, not away from it. Never let go of a line until you have firm hold of another one. And to keep the respect of the veterans: scorn the "lubber's hole" through the mast top platform, climbing instead the futtock shrouds outboard of the platform edge. After your first time aloft, "pay your footing" by treating the crew to rum.

Greenhands of all ages had to "cross the line" (the equator) and be welcomed into the brotherhood of the sea by King Neptune before they would be considered true seamen. Hazing ranged from being shaved with an iron barrel hoop to being forced to eat vile concoctions. After their rite of passage, they were graduated to the rank of "old salt."

Being salty did not ward off seasickness, fear, and loneliness, however. One homesick novice aboard *Arctic* wrote after only six days at sea:
Monday, October 24—the day was stormy I wish I were home of all the places on earth there is no place like home I wanted to go to sea and now I have got enough of it Sunday I laid in my bunk and cried. . . .

Even for the seasoned tar, shipboard life could be trying. A good night's sleep called for experience and ingenuity. On smaller vessels, the crew hung their hammocks wherever they could find a nook, the deck being favored on warm nights. On larger Indiamen, a sailor's home was his forecastle—"before the mast"—but in some ways the open deck was preferable. As one disgruntled crew member complained: "the uncomfortable air of the fore-castle—increased by the breath of sixteen men . . . and the stench of the vomit from the sick men—prevented me from sleeping much." He failed to mention the stench of pitch and bilgewater or the humid heat and damp cold of the cramped space. Vermin often infested the "donkey's breakfast" straw mattresses, and "ship fever" was often the result of the crowded and unsanitary conditions.

Hardest to stomach for a hard-working seaman was the poor food. An apprentice soon learned to inspect his rations for weevils and maggots before eating. Preserved food made up the bulk of his diet: salt pork and beef (called "salt junk" because of its resemblance to rope); dried fish; dried peas, rice, beans, or potatoes; and hardtack. This was supplemented by whatever fresh fish they caught and, if the captain was wise, "greens and salad . . . to keep off the scurvy." The cook, known as "doctor," did what he could at his cast iron or brick galley, occasionally treating the crew to lobscouse, a concoction of dried potatoes and peas mashed together with salt beef, hardtack, and water and cooked to a mush. The quality of such victuals was frequently the object of black humor. One seaman observed that meals included "stuff they call coffee made by pouring water on the grounds that are left from the master table . . . and biscuits that would make good protection for house roofs instead of slates . . . being much harder and consequently more durible."

Shipboard fare, however unpalatable, represented the least of the perils of the voyage. All too often during Salem's history, its citizens heard the town crier intone the words, "Lost, Lost, Lost." For those crewmen who were often aloft, a fall was the sword of Damocles hanging over every head. If a seaman went overboard in a storm, he usually had no hope of rescue. Capt. Richard Cleveland told of a young Norwegian sailor who "fell from the yard, struck his head against the main chains, and fell into the sea. He was seen but a moment, his head very bloody, and then disappeared."

There were the unseen dangers. Anyone who sailed the tropical regions ran a gauntlet of diseases. Among those who died a terrible death from "Yellow Jack," or yellow fever, was Capt. Nathaniel Hathorne, father of Nathaniel Hawthorne. On a moonless night, another vessel could glide silently out of the darkness on a collision course before anyone could react. With the fatalism that many sailors brought to their trade, a crewman on *William Schroder* of Salem wrote after one close encounter: "All that was said or thought of it was that David Jones did not get us this time, though we are consigned to his locker one of these days."

Every sailor dreaded seeing the stormy petrel, harbinger of a storm. Richard Cleveland describes his experience on *Aspasia,* sailing in gale winds off the west coast of Africa in 1806:

Under reduced sail we were making ten knots an hour . . . when a tremendous crash was heard, and at

Perils on the Sea

In the grip of a North Atlantic winter storm, the sturdiest wooden sailing vessel was a fragile thing indeed. Even hardened sailors aboard *Ulysses,* shown here, must have quaked as, decks awash with freezing water and two masts gone by the board, their ship was driven by a blinding snowstorm closer and closer to the surf they could hear pounding the banks of Cape Cod. No other profession was as dangerous during the decades of Salem's prominence, as attested to by the city's 400 widows among a population of less than 7,000 in 1783. Sailors likened being at sea to being in prison with the added possibility of drowning. Unfortunately, that was only one of a depressing litany of ways a sailor could meet an early end. He could be swept overboard at night and simply disappear. There was the daily danger of falling from the rigging to the deck far below. In southern latitudes especially, unseen enemies like malaria and yellow fever could carry a man off quickly. And the medical treatment on board sometimes only made a bad condition worse.

Capt. Richard Cleveland preferred the "ordinary perils of rocks and shoals . . . to . . . the greater ones of the cupidity and villany of man." Pirates haunted many corners of the world, waiting for careless prey. They often left no survivors. Just as dangerous were apparently friendly traders who could change instantly into fierce plunderers, like the Malays who, wielding their deadly *krises* (short swords), attacked the Salem East Indiaman *Friendship* in 1831 at Quallah Battoo in Sumatra, killing five men. Even more gruesome fates awaited the unwary. One Salem crew of 14, while gathering *beche-de-mer* (sea cucumbers or sea slugs) from the Fiji Islands for the China trade, was taken by cannibals. Thirteen were eaten. Terrifying as such dangers were, rocks and shoals remained a seaman's greatest enemy. While vessels did sink in deep water, whereabouts unknown, it was shallow water that crews feared most. Navigational error, poor visibility, uncharted rocks, or violent storms could bring a ship aground, where it broke up if the damage to the hull was severe enough. That is what happened to *Ulysses,* and to two other vessels, *Volusia* and *Brutus,* on February 22, 1803, the day after they had left Salem for Bordeaux. After the blizzard grounded the ships in the churning surf, most of the crewmen struggled ashore. But those farthest from shelter wandered the frigid beach all night in soaked clothes, and 87 of them froze to death.

In his "Narrative of Voyages and Travels," Capt. Amasa Delano listed the fates of the 60 crew members of Massachusetts *on its 1790 voyage to Canton. Some 25 years after the voyage, at least 48 had died—20 at sea by drowning, disease, accident, or murder by pirates. One was a slave in Algiers.*

the same moment the foremast was seen to be falling over to leeward. The vessel, no longer mindful of her helm, came up into the wind. The scene now for a few moments, was one of dismay. The darkness of the night, the roaring sea, the howling wind, the quick and sharp rolling of the vessel, unchecked by any sail, the thumping against the vessel of the spars which had fallen alongside, and which threatened mischief, and the difficulty of coming at the rigging, which held the spars, in order to cut it away, all combined to make our situation one of great perplexity.

Cleveland then described the efforts to ascend the mainmast head and cut away the rigging. The rolling of the ship caused the mast shrouds to slacken and then pull up tight with great force. One man trying to climb the ratlines was thrown off when the shroud tautened with a violent jerk, but was saved when he fell into the lowered mainsail. The crew finally cut away the wreckage of spars and rigging, rigged a jury mast, and continued the voyage.

Deadly as a storm at sea could be, a vessel was less likely to sink in the middle of the ocean than to run aground on a shoal or be carried to a sudden end against some rocky coast. Crews threading their way through the infamous straits of the East Indies spent days anticipating the terrible jolt of a submerged rock rending their hull. Nearby waters were no less dangerous. More Salem vessels wrecked off the Cape Hatteras graveyard or stormy Cape Cod than were lost in the legendary West Indian hurricanes. Perhaps most tragic were the vessels that had sailed to the Indies only to break up within sight of home on Salem Bay's submerged rocks, such as "Bowditch Ledge," named for the unfortunate vessels or captains who discovered them. Salem breathed easier when the Baker Island Lights, showing a safe passage, were installed in 1798.

Salem crews especially feared the human predators haunting the West Indies, the North African coast, and the East Indies. To the local rulers of these places, piracy was as legitimate a source of income as smuggling had been to American colonists before the Revolution, and they made scant distinction between trading partner and prey. A captain trading in Sumatra knew that the turbaned Malay traders he dealt with one day could convert their *proas* to pirate vessels the next and attack him after he left port.

LIST OF MEN'S NAMES, RANK, PLACES OF BIRTH, AND WHAT HAS BECOME OF THEM.

NAMES.	STATIONS.	PLACE OF BIRTH.	REMARKS.
Samuel Delano.	Carpenter.	Duxbury.	Now living.
William Trotter.	Boatswain,	England.	Living in the State of Vermont.
Edward Boden.	Gunner.	Beverly.	Dead.
Jonathan Stoddard.	Steward.	Boston.	Died at Macao in 1792.
Jonathan Winship.	Cooper.	New London.	Dead.
Matthew Cox.	Cabin Steward.	Boston.	Died at Canton in 1790.
Henry Anderson.	Carpenter's mate.	England.	Dead.
James Hurley.	do. do.	Boston.	Died in England.
Elias Parkman.	do. do.	Concord.	Living on Ponobscot River.
Jonathan Porter.	do. do.	Taunton.	Dead.
Charles Bowman.	Boatswain's mate.	England.	do.
John Harris.	do. do.	Sweden.	A slave in Algiers by the last accounts.
Roger Dyer.	Quarter Master.	Boston.	Died and thrown overboard off Cape Horn.
William Williams.	do. do.	Scotland.	Lost overboard off Jappan.
John Johnson.	do. do.	England.	Died on board an English Indiaman.
James Crowly.	do. do.	Ireland.	Murdered by the Chinese near Macao.
Charles Sobery.	Owner's Servant.	Boston.	Died on the passage from Batavia to Canton.
William Gorden.	Seaman.	Ireland.	Dead.
Nathaniel Butterfield.	do.	do.	do.
Alexander Martin.	do.	Virginia.	No knowledge of him.
Seth Stowell.	Seaman.	Hingham.	Was drowned at Whampoa in 1790.
Prospect Carpenter.	do.	Pembroke.	Dead.
George Green.	do.	England.	do.
William Martin.	do.	Rhode-island.	do.
John Wallis.	do.	Ireland.	do.
Jeremiah Chace.	do.	Cape Cod.	Died with the small pox in Whampoa in 1791.
William Bacon.	do.	Cambridge.	Dead.
John Collins.	do.	Salem.	do.
Thomas Magness.	do.	Scotland.	do.
William-Bacon, 2d.	do.	England.	No knowledge of him.
Jonathan Rogers.	do.	do.	Dead.
Dennis O' Flarrity.	do.	do.	do.
John Buffington.	do.	do.	do.
Charles Tredwell.	do.	Portsmouth N. H.	Living in New Hamshire.
Joseph Gruard.	do.	do.	No knowledge of him.
Thomas Lunt.	do.	do.	Living in New Hampshire.
Andrew Tombs.	do.	do.	No knowledge of him.
Humphrey Chadburn.	do.	do.	Shot and died at Whompoa in 1791.
John Wall.	do.	England.	Lost overboard off Jappan.
Larra Connor.	do.	Ireland.	Dead, murdered off Macao.
Benjamin Harryman.	do.	England.	Dead.
Robert Loviss.	do.	Marblehead.	do.
Jonathan Lovitt.	do.	Beverly.	Died at Whampoa in 1791.
James Fairsarvice.	do.	Boston.	do.
Malika Foot.	do.	do.	do.
John Tinker.	Seaman.	Cape Cod.	Dead.
Soseph Joplin.	do.	Salem.	do.
John Smith.	do.	England.	do.
John Bartlet.	do.	Boston.	do.
William Closs.	do.	England	do.
Benjamin Head,	do.	Boston.	do.
William Murphy.	do.	Ireland.	Murdered by the Chinese near Macao.
John Gregory.	Cook.	Boston.	Dead.
Lincoln.	do.	do.	do.
John Tracy.	Seaman.	England.	Died in India with the liver complaint.
James Barry.	do.	Boston.	No knowldge of him.
Bartholomew Englisby.	do.	do.	do.
John Symms.	do.	do.	do.
Samuel Tripe.	do.	Portsmouth N. H.	Drowned off Java Head, in 1790.
James Stackpole.	do.	Ireland.	Murdered by the Chinese off Macoa.
Nicholas Nicholson.	do.	Cape Cod.	Died with the leprosy at Macoa.

The above contains the names of all the crew that I have, a number of which I heard were dead,
but do not now the manner of their death.

Nathaniel Bowditch (1773-1838) was one of Salem's best minds and most respected citizens. His father was a captain who reportedly lost two vessels at sea. The family was often destitute, yet Nathaniel taught himself mathematics, astronomy, navigation, Latin, and several foreign languages before going to sea. From 1795-99 he made four voyages as captain's writer and supercargo, studying the arcane science of calculating longitude by determining the moon's position. Making countless observations and calculations, he discovered some 8,000 errors in the standard British navigational tables, so he published in 1802 *The New American Practical Navigator*, with corrected tables, information on winds, currents, and tides, mathematical instruction, and simplified formulas for "taking lunars." The same year he made his final voyage as captain of the ship *Putnam*, where he put his theories into practice. His book has been translated into a dozen languages and has remained the sailor's bible through more than 70 editions. For Bowditch's contributions to seafaring, the Boston Marine Society paid him tribute: "His intuitive mind sought and amassed knowledge, to impart it to the world in more easy forms."

In Bowditch's day, determining latitude was a relatively simple matter of measuring the sun's angle above the horizon by "shooting the sun" (see diagram) at noon. This was done with an octant like the one shown here, owned by Bowditch. Tables converted that figure for the day, month, and year into distance north or south of the equator. Determining longitude, the ship's distance east or west of the prime meridian at Greenwich, England, had long been a problem for navigators. Chronometers could tell a captain the exact time at Greenwich. The difference between the ship's time and Greenwich Mean Time could be converted into the distance from Greenwich. But chronometers were still too expensive and fragile for common use. Therefore, before Bowditch's work gave captains and crews a method of determining longitude by lunar angle, they relied on the ancient technique of "dead reckoning." After a ship left a port of known latitude and longitude, her new positions were plotted by determining the nautical miles (equal to one minute of latitude) traveled over a course set by compass. Distance equaled elapsed time multiplied by speed, which was measured with a chip log and reel **1**. A crew member threw the log overboard and counted the regularly-spaced knots in the rope as they were pulled over the stern during one turn of a 28-second log glass. This measurement was converted to nautical miles per hour (thus the term "knots"). Pegs inserted at each half-hour in the traverse board **2** recorded the time run on each dead reckoning course. Captains also practiced "parallel sailing," by which they simply

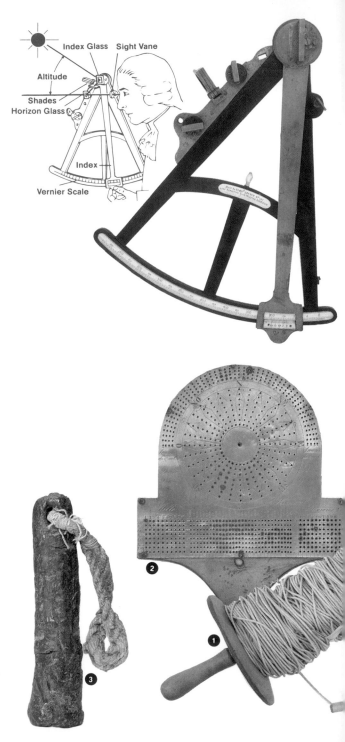

sailed north or south to the correct latitude, then followed it until they hit their destination. The sounding lead was another crucial instrument of navigation in shallow waters. A lead weight 3 was tied to a line marked in fathoms (six feet). "Heaving the lead" involved swinging the weight as far ahead of the vessel as possible, so it would be close to perpendicular when it reached the bottom, for an accurate reading of the depth. A plug of tallow retrieved bottom samples, which also helped to determine location.

The crew of the Salem ship *Friendship* paid dearly for dropping its guard. The vessel was anchored off Quallah Battoo at Sumatra in 1831. While Capt. Charles Endicott was ashore, the crew allowed a number of Malays on board. Once in position, they pulled out their *krises*—short steel or bone swords often made more deadly with poison—and attacked, killing five crew members who resisted.

With so many ways to die, it is not surprising that some mariners turned to the solace of drink. Every man looked forward to seeing the sun over the foreyard, when he received his "nooner" of grog. The small ration of watered rum did not inebriate, but was enough to take the edge off. Captains and mates also turned to alcohol, and more than a few respectable merchants had once been hard-drinking captains who liked to start the day with a thunder mug of punch—hot water and spices laced with rum. Once in port, the fraternity of New England captains gathered at every chance to wash the salt from their throats with liberal drafts of Madeira wine.

For some, the tedium could be an even stronger spur to drink. Progress was often maddeningly slow. A vessel beating in the wind's eye might make three miles in two days. Capt. Benjamin Hodges complained of the lack of "Society and Exercise." Weeks could pass without "speaking" another vessel, and there was little room to move about freely. Alcohol was for some the only escape from what Hodges called the "Blue Devils."

One temperate captain, outraged to find his first mate three sheets to the wind, entered in the permanent log: "The mate drunk all day." When the mate protested that this could ruin his career, the captain responded, "It was true, wasn't it?" Not about to let this go unrevenged, the mate entered in the log the next day: "The captain sober all day." His answer to the indignant captain: "It was true, wasn't it?"

Religion also helped anxious sailors, but it competed with superstition. Seamen were, in the words of Capt. Amasa Delano, "powerfully affected by the traditions which are handed down from generation to generation, concerning omens, charms, predictions, and the agency of invisible spirits." A captain, however, had to face the challenges of a voyage on a more rational basis. As Capt. Benjamin Crowninshield lamented in his log: "At 6 AM set Royals in

81

hopes to coax or Couzin a wind, but we are not profest Whitches 'tho from Salem."

The pressures on a captain were extraordinary. He had to sail a fine line between making good speed and bringing home intact the crew, vessel, and cargo. Some earned a reputation for "carrying on"— setting too much sail for the wind conditions. The temptation was particularly strong in the "Roaring Forties," the latitudes below 40°S where prevailing westerly gales could shorten a voyage to the Indian Ocean. But the area was also known for its sudden shifts in wind, and an overzealous captain could find his vessel "taken aback" and literally blown over as the price for carrying on.

A strong-minded captain was often frustrated. Though he was half a world away from Salem, he had to follow sailing orders with which he might strongly disagree. The latitude allowed captains varied with the shipowner for whom they sailed. Some, like Elias Hasket Derby, gave their captains great discretionary powers, expecting them to bend with the markets. Even so, cynical caution prevailed among some captains, who lived by the rule, "Obey orders if it breaks the owner."

Not so Benjamin Crowninshield, cousin to the famous Crowninshield brothers. The notoriously independent "Sailor Ben" left Salem aboard his cousins' ship *America* in July 1802, with emphatic orders to proceed to Sumatra for pepper. But the Crowninshield business agent at Isle de France (now Mauritius—a small island in the Indian Ocean) informed the captain that world pepper prices were declining while the market for coffee was on the rise. Breaking orders, Sailor Ben took his vessel to Mocha and purchased a shipload of coffee.

When *America* was sighted in Salem in June 1805, pepper had continued to fall and coffee was bringing excellent prices. The Crowninshields were praying that Sailor Ben had remained true to form. Unable to wait for the ship to dock, old George Crowninshield and his son Benjamin rowed out to meet Crowninshield. Approaching the vessel, one of them was sure he smelled coffee, but the other thought it only the galley pot brewing on deck. Finally, disregarding all marine etiquette, Benjamin shouted, "What's your cargo?"

"Pepper!" yelled back Sailor Ben, greatly amused

by his cousin's discomfort. Not fully appreciating the joke, the owner responded with an oath, but shouted with no small amount of satisfaction, "You lie! I smell coffee!" This time the captain had broken orders and was a hero. But the captain whose independence did not profit the owner would quickly find himself without a command.

No captain's job was completely secure. In bad times, when there were fewer commands available, some of the younger captains found themselves mates once again, pushing younger mates back to the forecastle. But while he had command, a successful captain's rank in Salem society was only slightly below that of a merchant. Many hoped to "swallow the anchor"—retire early from the sea and become merchants themselves. Not every captain, however, gathered enough capital to buy his own ships. Some joined the customs service upon retirement, but those positions were few. Capt. Thomas Webb was reduced to keeper of the prison ship anchored at Rust's Wharf during the War of 1812.

Many common seamen hoped to rise "through the hawse hole" to the rank of captain. Some, through outstanding performance, attained this goal without benefit of family connections. Henry Prince, cooper's apprentice, was 21 before he ever went to sea, yet within three years he had a command, became one of Salem's most prominent captains, and bought Elias Hasket Derby's house on Derby Street. But within Salem's deep-rooted hierarchy, such achievements were rare. More typical was John Prince, the boy who showed up on his Uncle Elias' doorstep, shipped aboard his vessels, and eventually commanded them.

The more daring boys being groomed as captains shipped as common seamen and lived the rough life of a sailor. This was done less out of egalitarian impulse than as a way to gain the hard practical knowledge of how a ship is run. Most, like Richard Cleveland, chose to room apart from the crew, "free from the vulgarity of the forecastle." These "ship's cousins" avoided the worst tasks of the regular crewman but still experienced some of the rigors and dangers of shipboard life.

No matter what his advantage at the start, a boy who showed no ability to handle a tough crew would never make captain. If a ship's company could be

Nathaniel Silsbee (1773-1850) was one of Elias Hasket Derby's most renowned captains. At 19 he was trusted with command of Derby's new ship Benjamin *on a voyage to India. His reputation as a sharp trader began on that venture when he earned a 100-percent profit for Derby. He became known as a strict captain who could get the job done. Buying greater and greater interests in the ships he sailed, he retired from the sea before the age of 30 to send out his own ships under other captains. He married Mary Crowninshield, sister of his close friend Jacob, whom he joined in politics when he was elected senator from Massachusetts.*

likened to a sovereign state, it was closer to the autocratic kingdoms of the Old World than American democracy. The captain's authority was supreme. On George Nichols' second voyage as captain, he called the crew together and told them what to expect: "Now, my men, I begin fair with you. If you do your duty faithfully and cheerfully, you shall say at the end of the voyage that it has been the pleasantest you ever made, but if you are unfaithful, I will feed you on shavings and sawdust." Though discipline on a merchantman was less harsh than on a naval vessel, offenses could still bring a flogging. Mutiny could be a capital offense.

Richard Cleveland, who in his memoirs seems a mild and tolerant man, had plenty of experience with hard crews, one of whose appearance "made it difficult to believe that most of them had not been familiar with crime. . . ." He proved as tough as his men. While *Beaver* was in a port in Peru, the mate refused to let the crew keep a jar of brandy. All hands left off work. Cleveland ordered the ringleader flogged, but when the mate started to lash him to the shrouds, the whole crew began moving toward Cleveland. He laid a rope across the deck, and, pistols in both hands, threatened to kill the first man across. No one crossed, he proceeded with the flogging, and, according to Cleveland, they were from that point "as orderly a crew as I could desire."

But even at sea, legal power had its practical limits. When a crew lost confidence in its captain, it became less efficient, costing him money and prestige. A captain who mistreated his crew or proved incompetent soon attained a reputation in the ports and pubs that made it difficult for him to recruit good seamen.

Captain Nichols' attitude toward his seamen was paternalistic:

I would here observe as regards sailors generally that I found them a much better class of people than I had supposed them to be; very kind-hearted, very generous and very easily governed if one only treats them kindly. . . . I had very strict regulations with regard to cleanliness, consequently my men were seldom sick, . . . but if at any time they were indisposed, I nursed them with as much care as I would my own children.

It was not unusual for the captain to serve as

medical officer, or "sawbones," dispensing medicines and performing surgery at sea. Nathaniel Silsbee, as a 19-year-old captain, had to amputate all the gangrened toes of his cook with a penknife.

Though money might have seemed poor compensation for danger, tedium, and homesickness, crews aboard Salem's merchantmen were relatively well-paid. For the 1811 voyage of his ship *Horace,* William Gray paid his captain $25 a month plus a five-ton "privilege," or cargo allowance for private adventures. Most captains also received "primage," one to eight percent of the profits on their cargo, and some were part owners of their vessel. The first and second mates were paid $25 and $23, with privileges. The seamen earned wages comparable to or better than land laborers—$20 a month for able-bodied, and $16 for ordinary seamen. Enterprising seamen supplemented their wages with their own adventures of rum, gin, and snuff.

While seamen were on voyages, their families received quarterly payments from the shipowner. This was a wise practice, as up to a third of a voyage was spent in port, and after weeks at sea, many seamen were drawn to places like the "flower boats"— floating brothels—on the Pearl River near Canton. But sailors did more than celebrate in port. Salem crew members showed great curiosity about South Seas cultures. After his first glimpse of New Zealand's Maori tribesmen, one crewman on *Tarquin* observed that they were a "stout robust treacherous voracious gluttinous naked set of wretches" and "regular Yankees for trade." Salem captains and crews lived up to their own reputation for trade, carrying back the artifacts and natural objects that made up the core of the East India Marine Society collections.

As generations of Essex County youths served their time before the mast, they brought back an easy familiarity with faraway places that enhanced and shaped the culture of Salem. For those sailors who chose to return to the sea, the lure of their calling is summed up in the words of Captain Cleveland, who conceded that the "hardships and privations of a seaman's life . . . |are| . . . greater than those of any other . . . ," but added, "if my life were to be passed over again, I should pursue the same course."

To Catch the Wind: The Ships

Elias Hasket Derby sent his highly successful ex-privateer Grand Turk *on the first Salem voyage to the East.*

This painting of Grand Turk *is from a bowl given to Captain Ebenezer West by Pinqua, the Canton merchant with whom West dealt. The 300-ton ship was large for a Salem vessel of the time and still well-armed. Another Derby ship,* Mount Vernon **(left),** *was one of Salem's fastest vessels.*

Since that distant time when someone first stood up in a boat, spread his arms, and let the breeze fill his clothing, the sight of a wind-driven vessel gliding over the water has been a basic image of human culture. Hewing trees into hulls and masts, weaving plant fiber into sails and cordage, civilizations have harnessed the wind to trade their products, share technology, and migrate over the seas.

Sail reached its culmination in 19th-century naval and commercial vessels—a marriage of beauty and utility rarely matched by steam. In port cities like Salem, the pride of the community was embodied in the ships riding in its harbor. Many of Salem's citizens were involved in building, fitting, and supplying them. More than a few had interests in the vessels. When they watched one leave the wharf with a large common investment and 10 or 15 young men, they were watching their future.

At its peak in 1807, Salem's fleet numbered some 200 vessels. The most famous were known around New England and in the world's ports: *Herald, Margaret, Belisarius, Franklin, Hercules, Hope.* This fleet had grown from the three tiny fishing shallops built by Robert Moulton for the colonists in 1629. The shipbuilding industry grew rapidly during the 17th century, rivaling the fisheries by the 1660s as the town's leading industry. By the 1680s, 40 ketches plied the fishing and coasting trades and four ships and two barks were sailing to the West Indies and Europe. With few exceptions, these vessels were Salem-built.

The early marine "artificers" naturally looked to England for guidance. To ensure the quality of Massachusetts vessels, the legislature required that prospective English buyers send over "some able man to survey the work and workmen from time to time." The shipwrights of Salem and other New England ports learned so well from England's masters that London shipbuilders petitioned the Lords of

The Shipbuilder's Craft

An East Indiaman slipping down the ways from a Salem shipyard was the result of a highly cooperative enterprise. The products of at least 20 crafts were displayed in the finished vessel. King of the yard was the shipwright—the man to praise or blame for the final product. He designed the vessel, watched the budget, and supervised construction. In some cases he provided capital or even owned the yard. Besides the 20 or so "mechanics" employed on each ship, he contracted with artisans to provide components he could not produce in the yard.

In the days before plans were common, Salem shipwrights carved a "half model," or "lift model" (inset). This was a half hull that could be separated into sections (lifts) to aid workers in transferring its contours to patterns drawn on the "mold loft" floor. Following the patterns, hewers shaped the frames with broad axes and adzes. They worked with naturally curved "compass timber" (right), in which the grain followed the shape of the desired section. For structural members and planking, white oak was preferred for its strength and resistance to rot. Masts and spars, usually of white pine, were pickled in salt water ponds to preserve their resilience. The keel, made of two or more pieces "scarfed" together, was laid down on large blocks. The

Crowd watches launching of Fame *from Becket's shipyard in 1802. Painting by George Ropes, Jr.*

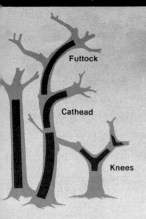

Futtock

Cathead

Knees

stem and stern posts were attached at either end, and rib-like frames were raised. A good crew could attach the planking to the skeleton at the rate of two to five levels, or "strakes," a day. Borers drilled holes through the planks and frame, and the fastener drove in the large wooden tree nails, or "trunnels." After caulkers (the highest paid of the mechanics) sealed the planking seams with tarred hemp fibers, called oakum, joiners smoothed and planed the surface and coated the hull with a mixture of resin, sulphur, and tallow to repel boring teredo worms and barnacles. Once the hull was in the water and the planking swelled, it was reasonably watertight, although some leaking was expected in every wooden vessel. A well-built ship was expected to last 20 years, but many were in service even longer, sometimes up to 30 years.

The Efficient Merchantman

After a ship was launched, its masts were "stepped"— inserted through the decks with a crane and anchored to the keelson—and fittings and equipment were installed. A typical Salem East Indiaman was about 100 feet stem to stern, with a breadth of 28 feet amidships. These vessels were small compared to the great multi-masted ships that followed. The main yard of the five-masted *Preussen* (1902) was as long as the Salem ship *George.*

Most Indiamen followed the layout shown here: **1** davit; **2** taffrail; **3** quarterdeck; **4** wheel; **5** binnacle (houses compass); **6** companionway

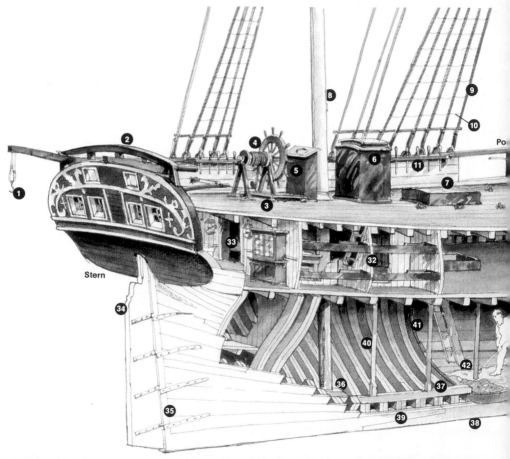

Stern

Ropewalks of a thousand or more feet made the cordage used on a ship. Ropemakers produced a "neutral" rope by balancing the tension created by twisting. Combed hemp was attached to a revolving hook and spun into yarn. Several yarns were then at- tached to separate hooks and twisted together in the oppo- site direction to form mar- line. Three of these were in turn twisted together, again in the opposite direction, to make rope. Three ropes were twisted still again into anchor cable.

(ladder access); **7** hatch; **8** mizzenmast; **9** main shrouds; **10** ratlines; **11** pinrails and belaying pins; **12** mainmast; **13** fife rail; **14** pump; **15** foremast; **16** knightheads; **17** bowsprit; **18** gammoning; **19** cathead; **20** anchor; **21** anchor cable windlass;

22 forecastle; **23** 'tween decks; **24** wale; **25** scuppers; **26** fake gunports; **27** boarding ladder; **28** main rail; **29** bulwarks; **30** chain plates; **31** deadeyes; **32** ship's officers' cabins; **33** captain's cabin; **34** rudder; **35** stern post; **36** mast step; **37** keelson; **38** keel;

39 scarf joint; **40** stanchion; **41** hold; **42** ballast; **43** hanging knee; **44** frames; **45** planking (strakes); **46** coating of tallow, resin, and sulphur; **47** copper sheathing; **48** stem.

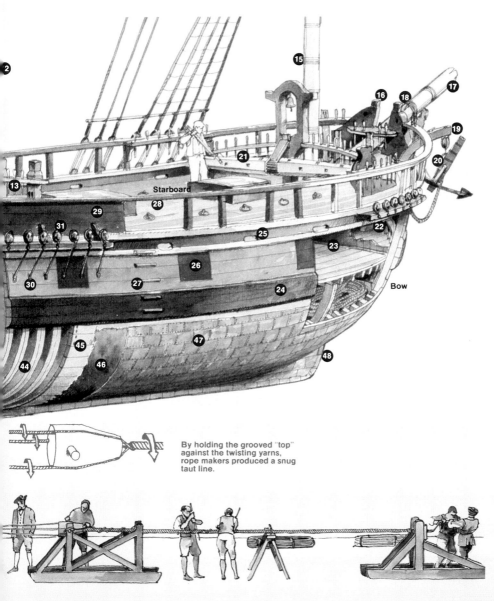

By holding the grooved "top" against the twisting yarns, rope makers produced a snug taut line.

Sails and Rigging

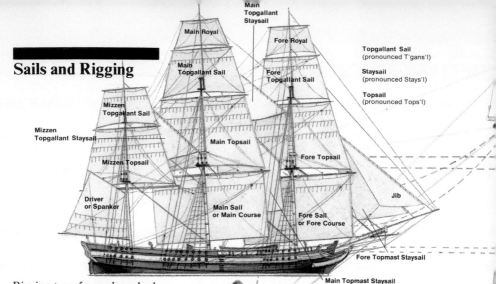

Main Topgallant Staysail

Main Royal

Fore Royal

Main Topgallant Sail

Fore Topgallant Sail

Mizzen Topgallant Sail

Topgallant Sail
(pronounced T'gans'l)

Staysail
(pronounced Stays'l)

Topsail
(pronounced Tops'l)

Mizzen Topgallant Staysail

Main Topsail

Mizzen Topsail

Fore Topsail

Driver or Spanker

Main Sail or Main Course

Fore Sail or Fore Course

Jib

Fore Topmast Staysail

Main Topmast Staysail

Rigging transformed a naked hull into a graceful sailing vessel. Given a skillful crew, a captain could play the aerial maze of sails, spars, and lines like an instrument, tuning his vessel to weather and sea conditions, capturing as much wind as he dared without overstraining the masts. The materials had to be good to withstand such pressure. Tough Baltic hemp was used for the tar-coated standing rigging—the shrouds and stays that guyed the masts. Sails were hoisted or moved with the untarred running rigging, which passed through blocks above and was made fast on the belaying pins below.

To shorten, or reef, a sail, sailors below cast off the halyards to lower the yard and hauled a section of the sail up to the yard, while others above gathered the sail and tied it with the attached reef points. Furling involved gathering the entire sail to the yard, where it was secured with short ropes, or "gaskets."

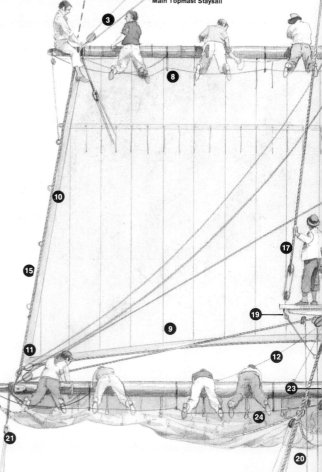

92

Sailing vessel types were identified by the number of masts and whether their sails were square-rigged (perpendicular to the keel) or fore-and-aft. Square-rigged vessels with three masts were the only ones properly called "ships."

1 main crosstrees; 2 main topmast; 3 lifts; 4 halyard; 5 topsail yard; 6 footropes; 7 main topsail; 8 head of sail; 9 foot of sail; 10 leech of sail; 11 clew; 12 buntlines; 13 reef tackle; 14 reef points; 15 bolt rope; 16 mainmast cap; 17 topmast shrouds; 18 main top; 19 futtock shrouds; 20 sheet line; 21 braces; 22 lower yard; 23 parrel; 24 main sail or course; 25 main shrouds; 26 main mast.

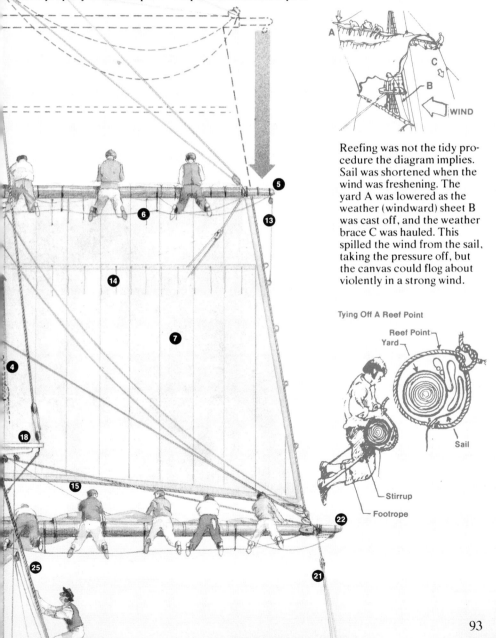

WIND

Reefing was not the tidy procedure the diagram implies. Sail was shortened when the wind was freshening. The yard A was lowered as the weather (windward) sheet B was cast off, and the weather brace C was hauled. This spilled the wind from the sail, taking the pressure off, but the canvas could flog about violently in a strong wind.

Tying Off A Reef Point

Reef Point

Yard

Sail

Stirrup

Footrope

93

A merchant's choice of vessels depended on the amount of cargo, length of the voyage, and kinds of waters and weather the vessel would encounter. A square-rigger could put up more sail, and thus had the advantage of speed and power with a following wind. But a fore-and-aft rig needed fewer crewmen and could maneuver more deftly, giving it the edge in confined areas. A vessel that combined the two, such as a bark (with mizzenmast fore-and-aft rigged), gained in versatility. **Two-masted brigs 1** carried less cargo than ships, drew less water, and could enter more harbors and rivers. **Ketches 2**, the favored fishing and coasting vessels of the 17th century, were essentially small ships without a foremast. Fore-and-aft rigged **Schooners 3** were excellent coastal or deepwater traders. **Sloops 4** served as small fishing boats and short-run carriers.

No vessel could sail straight into the wind, although a fore-and-aft rig could sail a few points closer than a square-rigger. When a vessel had to sail into the wind, it "tacked," or sailed a zigzag course as close as possible to the direction from which the wind blew. A large ship with 12 square sails might take 15 minutes to come about. The crew let go the sheets and hauled on the braces to pivot the great yards, their sails flapping loudly, until the wind came over the opposite bow, the sails filled, and the ship headed off on its new tack. Sometimes a vessel without sufficient headway failed to come about, or "missed stays," and it drifted astern "in irons" until it fell off the wind for another try.

94

Trade in 1724 to restrict colonial shipbuilding. By the Revolution, however, colonial yards were launching one-third of all commercial vessels used by Great Britain. Two-thirds of colonial-built vessels were constructed in New England shipyards.

Yankee shipwrights would no doubt have claimed native ability as the reason for their success, but some of it must be attributed to their location near an ample supply of raw materials: iron, flax, oak, and "big stick" white pine for masts. British shipbuilders had to compete with American yards that could produce good vessels on a smaller investment.

Numerous small shipyards dotted the riverbanks and seacoast of New England, with shipbuilding centers on the North River and the lower Merrimack from Haverhill to Newburyport. Boston and Charlestown had large shipyards, but after the Revolution they concentrated on ship repair and naval construction. Until 1790, when Salem's first sizable sailcloth and iron factories were established, its shipbuilders turned out mostly small fishing and coasting vessels, while large brigs and ships were generally built elsewhere. Even in the Federalist period, the largest ships were often built in other ports, especially Medford on the Mystic River. While Salem never produced the largest vessels, its East Indiamen, built to carry valuable cargoes from the Indies, were the equal of any in quality.

It was relatively easy for a shipwright with a little capital to establish a yard. Any shoreline site with access to materials, fresh water, and water deep enough for launching could serve as a shipyard, but a sheltered location with a slight incline to ease launching was preferred. One of the earliest in Salem, up the South River on Ruck's Creek, was "Knocker's Hole," so named for the incessant pounding of the caulkers' mallets. Larger yards were located near the mouth of the river and on the shore of the outer harbor.

Salem shipowners owned vessels built throughout New England, but preferred to have them built by local shipwrights. Many merchants had a fair knowledge of shipbuilding and liked to keep a close eye on the progress of their vessel. Once a merchant or group of merchants had selected a shipbuilder, they drew up a contract specifying the types of materials to be used, such as "good sound White Oak timber,"

When wheels replaced tillers and whipstaffs (vertical levers) in the early 18th century, the helmsman's job was made much easier. Circular motion was converted into back-and-forth rudder action by a series of pulleys.

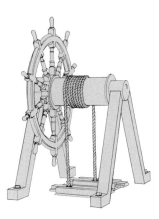

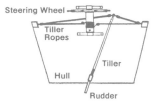

The carpenter's tools were as important to a ship as a seaman's marlin spike or the captain's octant. After the ship left home port her continuing seaworthiness depended on the carpenter's skill.

Barnacles and seaweed could slow a vessel by a third. The easiest way to clean a vessel's bottom was to careen and bream it (below), that is, heel

it over and burn off the encrusted growths. After the brig Eunice (right) *had been careened, she became stranded on the beach and had to be "casked" (encased in a huge wooden cylinder) and rolled into the water. Careening was also done for caulking and*

with stiff penalties for corner-cutting. Rather than submitting plans, most shipwrights of the period carved a wooden scale-model of one side of the hull. The carpenters derived the actual dimensions of the vessel from this "half-model."

The vessels they built emerged from a scene of ordered clutter. The yard was awash in woodchips, and piles of lumber were everywhere, with more arriving on ox-drawn carts. The pungent smells of tar and newly-cut pine, fir, and oak hung in the air. Skilled tradesmen—carpenters, sawyers, hewers, plankers, dubbers, painters, caulkers—climbed over hulls in varying stages of completion. Every vessel started with the keel—the all-important backbone. The keel was "scarfed" together from several shorter pieces and laid on large blocks near the water. Carpenters hewed the stem and stern posts and the curved floors and futtocks that were pieced together with wooden or iron dowels to form the frames. At the cry of "frame up!" everyone helped to position each frame on the keel and push it upright. Like sailors hauling on a halyard, they sang chanteys to make the work easier, and like their seafaring brothers, they expected a ration of grog to break up the day.

The curved ribs, braced with cross beams and angled knees, formed a strong, resilient skeleton. The thin planks that would give it a light but tough skin were produced at the sawpit, the top man inching across a beam laid over a hole as he pushed and pulled the saw, while the man in the pit worked under a shower of sawdust. With the planks, carpenters sheathed the sides and laid the deck. After caulking, the sides were scraped and coated with sulphur, resin, and tallow to make the hull watertight and to repel teredo worms. These long worms, which sounded "not unlike a multitude of borers with augers" according to Captain Cleveland, could honeycomb a hull in weeks.

At this point, the structure resting on the ways was still an inert hull, which would be made seaworthy by a band of craftsmen: Blockmakers, windlassmakers, anchor smiths, carvers, sailmakers, blacksmiths, pumpmakers, boatbuilders, sparmakers, joiners, instrument makers, and ropemakers. Much of their work was performed after the launching.

Each time a new hull touched water, the people of Salem reenacted a central ceremony of community life. Schools were closed, shops were shuttered, and crowds gathered hoping to witness a well-executed ride down the ways. After a few words from the owner, workers knocked out the restraints with sledge hammers and the vessel slowly slipped into the water to music, waving flags, and cheers. One resident described a vessel's "final shivering slide into the sea, and then after making the final plunge, rising majestically and settling down like a swan on the surface of the water." Not every launch was as stirring, however. When Enos Briggs signaled his men to launch the second *Grand Turk*, the huge vessel moved a few inches and ground to a stop. Again and again this happened, as the vessel took four embarrassing, anticlimactic days to launch.

Briggs, however, became the most celebrated of all Salem shipwrights. He already had a good reputation in Pembroke when Elias Hasket Derby brought him to Salem in 1790 to build *Grand Turk*, at 560 tons the largest American vessel of the day. Built next to Derby Wharf, its bowsprit reached over Derby Street. Briggs produced a series of large, fast Indiamen for Derby at his shipyard on Stage Point: *John, Three Sisters, Eliza*. He also built a number of well-known vessels for other owners: *Belisarius* for George Crowninshield, *Frances* and *Glide* for Joseph Peabody, and *Friendship* for Benjamin Hodges and George Nichols. His most famous was the frigate *Essex*, built by public subscription in 1799 and the largest vessel ever produced in Salem.

One of the earliest shipyards in Salem was that of John Becket, established in the mid-17th century next to Maj. John Turner's house with seven gables. The Becket family operated the yard continuously into the 19th century. Most renowned of the Becket shipbuilders was sixth-generation Retire Becket, the last of his line. "Tirey" built a number of Derby's and Crowninshield's famous vessels, starting with Derby's *Recovery*, the first American vessel to visit Arabia. *Mount Vernon, Fame*, the fourth *America, Herald*, and *Cleopatra's Barge* were products of the Becket yard.

Salem's larger ships in the elite Indies trade were its best known, but for much of its history, the port's fleet consisted of more modest vessels. In the early days, when Salem's trade was in its infancy and the town depended on its fishing industry, "the primitive

coppering, but it was expensive, dangerous, and time-consuming. To avoid it, Salem in 1824 built the Nation's first marine railroad.

Vessels mounted on cradles were pulled on tracks into the shipyard by horse or steam. If the vessel was small enough, men could do it with capstans and winches.

Salem's Armed Traders

Salem's ships carried guns as well as goods. Valuable cargoes made tempting prizes for pirates, and most captains routinely armed their vessels with small cannon and often a few wooden guns to make the vessel appear more formidable. When Salem was drawn into larger historical conflicts, every ship clearing the wharves was ready for battle, either as a predator or potential prey. When the French Revolutionaries warred with England, Amer-

ican neutral carriers were attacked by privateers and warships of both countries. The resulting undeclared sea war between France and America in 1798-99 was the setting for a famous series of battles involving Elias Hasket Derby's ship *Mount Vernon*. Commanded by Derby's son Hasket, the fast vessel sailed for Europe in 1799 on her maiden trading voyage carrying 20 guns and a letter-of-marque to take French prizes. Soon after reaching the Span-

Salem's Revolutionary privateer Mohawk *and a privateer ensign.*

ish coast in an amazing 17 days, *Mount Vernon* met a fleet of 50 sail that Derby took for British. But as one of them approached she raised French colors and fired. Derby returned a broadside and fled, followed by two French frigates that chased him for 24 hours before breaking off. On the next day a large French privateer attacked (shown here), but Derby beat her off. Shortly thereafter, *Mount Vernon* was again seemingly out-matched by a French privateer. But, in Derby's words to his father, "He came so near our broadsides as to allow our six-pound grape to do execution handsomely." The vessel struck her colors, but Derby declined to take her, writing that "it was satisfaction to flog the rascal in full view of the English fleet."

Salem's Contribution to the U.S. Navy

While Salem's commercial vessels put the port on the map, one of its most famous ships was the U.S. Frigate *Essex,* the only warship Salem's shipyards ever produced and the bane of British commercial vessels in the War of 1812. In 1798 the young U.S. government, needing ships to fight its undeclared sea war with France, asked several seaports to contribute to the cause, With almost $75,000 raised by subscription from Salem mer-

Capture of Essex *by British warships, 1814.*

chants and citizens, master shipbuilder Enos Briggs built an 850-ton frigate using all Essex-county materials. Donated to the fledgling navy in 1799, *Essex* was by all accounts extremely fast and "as fine a ship of her size as graces the American Navy," according to a Boston paper. *Essex* saw no combat in the conflict, but was sent around the Cape of Good Hope for escort duty, making her the first U.S. warship to enter the Indian Ocean. She spent the next decade protecting U.S. shipping from Mediterranean pirates.

In the War of 1812, *Essex*, commanded by Capt. David Porter and carrying 46 guns, became the first American vessel to capture a British warship. *Essex* took eight more British ships, then ventured into the Pacific, the first U.S. naval vessel to do so. She virtually wiped out the British whaling fleet off South America, spurring an enraged British Admiralty to send two warships in 1814 to stop *Essex*. Although Porter's frigate was outgunned and already crippled by the loss of a mast, he chose to confront them near Valparaiso, Chile. *Essex* put up a long defense (inset), but was reduced to a shattered hulk, with 58 of the crew of 255 killed. Despite the loss, Porter and the crew were hailed as heroes for the damage *Essex* had inflicted on British commerce.

Bearers of a Proud Name

The tradition of christening U.S. vessels *America* was upheld by the Crowninshields of Salem, who gave the name to four commercial vessels spanning Salem's golden age from independence to the War of 1812. The first was ironically the last British vessel taken in the Revolution — the 400-ton *Pompey* captured by the Derby privateer *Grand Turk*. George Crowninshield bought her in 1783 and renamed her *America* (below). His sons Jacob and Benjamin took the next *America,* again bought from Derby, on a highly profitable voyage to India in 1795 that laid the foundation for the Crowninshield fortune. They traded her two years later for the French frigate *Blonde,* which became *America* number 3. The fast, well-built ship made several profitable voyages in the pepper trade, but her 700-ton hull was too large to get close to Crowninshield's wharf. The family sold her back to France in 1803. They had Retire Becket build *America* number 4, at 473 tons one of the largest American-built merchantmen of the time and reputedly the fastest. This ship helped the Crowninshields dominate the pepper trade for two years, but it was as a privateer in the War of 1812 that she was best remembered. Her hull was shortened, razeed, and given solid oak sides, and she was rigged with a huge spread of sail, making her even faster (13 knots) than before. With

24 guns and a highly trained crew of 150, she was the most successful privateer of the War of 1812 (inset), taking 26 British prizes worth $1.1 million. But *America's* end was inglorious. After her last privateering voyage in 1814, she languished at Crowninshield wharf until 1831, when the hull was sold at auction.

The privateer America *chasing* Princess Elizabeth, *1814.*

Schooner Baltick, *45 tons, 1763*

Ship George, *328 tons, 1814*

Ship Belisarius, *209 tons, 1794*

Brig Leander, *223 tons, 1821*

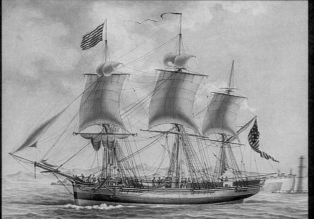
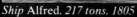

Ship Alfred, *217 tons, 1805*

Ship St. Paul, *463 tons, 1833*

Hermaphrodite Brig Elizabeth, *185 tons, 1842*

Bark Witch, *210 tons, 1854*

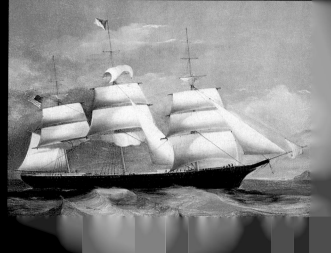

Pages 104-105: *For Salem shipowners, their vessels were objects of sentiment and pride as well as the source of their fortunes. They were often named after family members, and like honored ancestors, were portrayed for posterity. Among the best of the marine artists was Antoine Roux, who painted Salem ships, such as the Crowninshields'* America, *in Marseilles harbor. Italian artist Michele Felice Cornè, painter of* Mount Vernon, *moved to town and taught young Salem artists. One of his pupils was deaf and dumb George Ropes, who painted the famous view of Crowninshield Wharf showing a number of Salem ships (page 48). The streaming "homeward bound pennants" atop some of the depicted vessels were one foot long for every man on board. The number of stars they carried showed how many months the vessel had been at sea.*

Settlers did the principal part of their business in Shallops [of] 40 tons," according to Reverend Bentley. Shallops ranged from small, open or partially decked boats fitted with oars and a fore-and-aft spritsail or lugsail, to two-masted decked vessels.

As the fishing and trading industries became more specialized in the 17th century, sloops of 25 to 50 tons, and "trading ketches"—square-rigged vessels with main- and mizzenmasts—were the preferred craft. Ketches, ranging from 20 to 100 tons with a small hold, were well suited for voyages to the West Indies. By the early 18th century, Salem merchants still used the ketch, but increasingly employed the fore-and-aft rigged schooner for fishing and the coasting trade, and larger, square-rigged, two-masted brigs for ventures to Europe and the West Indies.

As Salem's trade expanded, so did the size of its trading vessels, although on average the vessels of Salem and Boston were smaller than those of many other ports, especially Philadelphia and those in Europe. During Salem's prime, in the years between the Revolution and the War of 1812, its brigs were typically 100 to 150 tons capacity and 60 to 90 feet long. Ships measured 200 to 300 tons and 75 to 100 feet. The largest East Indiamen averaged 330 tons, 99 feet long, with a breadth of 28 feet. Salem vessels were larger after the Revolution, but all ships of that period were small by later standards, and in 1795, at the height of his prosperity, Elias Hasket Derby's entire fleet of six ships, one bark, four brigs, two ketches, and a schooner still totaled less tonnage than the 1852 clipper ship *Sovereign of the Seas*.

Salem's vessels were held to their modest dimensions by hard economic constraints. In 1795 Derby sold *Grand Turk* to a New York firm because he considered the ship "much too large for our Port and the method of our trade." A ship so large held too much cargo, glutting the market. Small craft were also easier to handle and financially less risky, ensuring that the owner followed Sir Thomas More's dictum: "a wise marchant never adventures all his goodes in one shippe." They drew less water and thus were safer and had access to more ports and more goods. Finally, the size of vessels intended for Salem merchants was limited by the shallowness of their own harbor.

Salem vessels, and those of other northern ports,

tended to be slow compared to the early clipper-type vessels of the Delaware River and Chesapeake Bay. Their sluggish performance—a speed of nine knots off-the-wind was considered fast for a Salem or Boston vessel—was a result of their bluff, "cod's head" bows and chunky lines. Indiamen pushed the sea out of their way rather than slicing through it. Such a design was considered safer, but economics was the real shaper of the hull. The rounded barrel-bottoms added precious cargo space and allowed vessels to rest on the floor of Salem harbor at low tide. One exception to Salem's "tub school" of ship construction was Enos Briggs' ketch *Eliza*, which showed a curved stem and hollow water-lines. *Eliza* was a failure for her owners, who were impressed with her speed but not with her cargo capacity. Profits were made by packed holds, not record runs.

After the war of 1812, in which the fast clipper-type vessels proved successful privateers, that philosophy began to change. A group of Salem carpenters, thrown out of work by the war, built the privateer *George* with sharp lines. The war ended before *George* saw service, so they converted her to a merchantman and sold her to Joseph Peabody. She became his most famous ship, winning renown for her rapid runs to Calcutta, and setting an example for other shipbuilders in the postwar years. *George* also became known as the "Salem School Ship," with 45 of her crew members graduating to captain and 26 to mate.

Though sailing vessels increased their speed, and the true clippers of the mid-century were even faster, they were all overtaken by history and by steam. The great multi-masted ships, barks, and schooners put up a good fight against the steamers late in the century, but they had to bypass Salem's shallow harbor. By the end of the century only small coasting schooners were still visiting Salem.

Salem's great sailing vessels were icons of the Nation's preindustrial youth. Their taut sails and graceful lines embodied the port's energy, its elegance, its contribution to American growth. They also generated the capital later invested in the steam-powered vessels and industries that took the wind out of their sails. So it was sadly ironic when *Mindoro*, the last square-rigger registered in Salem, was towed from Derby Wharf in 1897 to become a coal barge.

The figurehead, traditionally believed to protect the crew, helped give a ship her identity and character. Shown here is the earliest known American figurehead, thought to have been carved around 1800 by Salem architect and wood-carver Samuel McIntire.

Bordeaux to Sumatra: Salem's World Trade

*Grand Turk's historic voyage ended with her arrival at the Chinese port of Canton in September 1786. Captain Ebenezer West found there the valuable China teas he had sought. Supercargo William Vans bought 500 chests of Bohea, Hyson, Congo, and Souchong, carried 800 miles from the inland hills (**left**) on sampans and on porters' backs. Vans proudly recalled years later in his autobiography, "I made a great voyage, bringing home to Salem, three capitals for the one I carried out."*

Salem embraced the world. No port was too distant, no waters too dangerous. Some of its seafaring citizens knew cities like Bombay and Nagasaki better than Boston and New York. Salem had been a prosperous port for a century and a half before it ventured beyond the Cape of Good Hope, but its flowering came in the wake of vessels pioneering the Eastern routes and opening markets to American trade.

The Indies trade put Salem on the world map, giving the town its style and character. It was a small port, but one that held its own in world markets with the large merchantmen of the East India Company fleets. Indeed, so familiar were Salem vessels in the Indies that some traders regarded "Salem" as a sovereign nation along with Great Britain and the Netherlands. The port took pride in its special place in world trade, affirming its connection with the Indies in the city's motto: "To the Farthest Port of the Rich East."

The great expansion of Salem's trade in the post-Revolutionary years was a matter of necessity. Salem's merchants knew they had to break out of the old patterns and compete for trade in distant ports. Elias Hasket Derby led the way by sending the first American vessel to Russia. *Light Horse* cleared for St. Petersburg in June 1784 with a cargo of sugar. Her return brought hemp and iron for the reviving shipbuilding industry. While the voyage was unprofitable because the Russians preferred bills of exchange to American goods, *Light Horse* was the bellwether of the lucrative Baltic trade.

As new markets followed in Africa, the Indies, and the Far East, Salem's web of trade routes reached virtually every corner of the world. Adventurous merchants and captains were especially drawn to China, whose tea, shipped in East India Company vessels, had caused so much resentment in the American colonies. Now John Adams was urging American

Sandalwood was one of the few products the Chinese wanted from Westerners. The wife of Capt. William Cleveland painted this watercolor of sandalwood being loaded at Timor in the East Indies in 1830.

Sandalwood carving portrays two Chinese men smoking opium, another trade good that found a market in Canton.

merchants to take away some of John Bull's tea trade. Again, Derby was the first New Englander to take up the challenge. His *Grand Turk*, a large, fast ex-privateer refitted as an Indiaman under the command of Capt. Jonathan Ingersoll, headed the procession of New England vessels to the East with her voyage to Cape Town in March 1785. Hoping to persuade a British East Indiaman to "break bulk" and sell some of its tea, Ingersoll met Samuel Shaw, supercargo on *Empress of China*, returning to New York from the first American voyage to China. On returning home, he described Shaw's rich cargo to Derby.

Derby was already contemplating such a venture. *Grand Turk*, commanded by the 27-year-old ex-privateersman Ebenezer West, left Salem again that December for Isle de France. *Grand Turk* was the first American ship to stop there, but West found little demand for his rum, rice, butter, flour, and fish. While he was selling the cargo, he was approached by a Frenchman who wanted to charter space on *Grand Turk* to carry a cargo to Canton. West agreed, hoping to find a profitable cargo there. He staked his career on this move, as *Grand Turk* was not insured beyond Isle de France and would be entering alien waters with only crude charts. The vessel was the first from America to try the dangerous Straits of Malacca at Sumatra.

West made it past the straits' pirates and natural hazards. On his arrival at the China coast in September 1786, he learned that his ship was the first from New England to reach China. Turning a profit, however, would be no easier than the voyage. Complex regulations and ancient custom surrounded all business transactions in Canton. Before foreigners reached Canton, their vessel was boarded by a Chinese pilot at Macao at the mouth of the Pearl River and sailed by him up to Whampoa, still 12 miles downriver from Canton.

There they were met by the Emperor's "Celestial Representative," the customs inspector, or "Hoppo." Direct Yankee traders learned to negotiate the treacherous waters of "cumshaw and measurements," a ceremony of subtlety, discretion, and unspoken agreements. To tonnage fees were added "cumshaw duty," which was the Hoppo's tip (some said bribe), the "opening barrier fee," and several other administrative duties, all of which totaled almost $3,500 for

Grand Turk. Official business over, the Hoppo gracefully accepted his "sing-song," usually cuckoo clocks or mechanical toys, for which he would insist on paying a token amount.

The cargo, accompanied by the officers and supercargo only, was moved on sampans up the river to Canton harbor, where it was maneuvered through bamboo-covered houseboats, junks, and lacquered tea-deckers and unloaded at the "factories." All "New People" were restricted to these warehouses and apartments in a walled waterfront area outside the city. Business was conducted through one of 10 or 12 Chinese merchants who controlled the warehouses, or "hongs," in which goods were stored. These hong merchants also guaranteed the foreigners' fees and were responsible for their behavior. For *Grand Turk* and many subsequent Salem vessels, the hong merchant Pinqua served as the go-between. West's supercargo William Vans purchased from Pinqua over 500 chests of four varieties of tea, porcelain, and cassia, called "Chinese cinnamon."

On her return to Salem Harbor in May 1787, *Grand Turk* was surrounded by smaller boats, salutes were fired in her honor, and crowds marveled at the cargo that brought Derby a profit of between 100 and 200 percent. Thus the China trade was opened to New England. American merchants soon made the right connections and established a reputation for square dealing and rapid loading and unloading, often enabling them to undercut prices offered by the European East India Companies for luxury cargoes.

As the vessels of other Salem merchants like William Gray began to appear at Whampoa, Derby expanded his Eastern trade network. In 1787, he sent his son Elias Hasket, Jr., a 22-year-old Harvard graduate, to manage the family's Eastern affairs from Isle de France. The island's Port Louis was the only French port open for unrestricted trade to foreign vessels, and it became a major center for Eastern goods, drawing speculators from around the world. The island became Salem's major trade center in the 1790s, with a tenth of all U.S. vessels calling there between 1786 and 1800 belonging to Derby.

On his arrival, Hasket sold *Grand Turk* and purchased two more ships, *Sultana* and *Peggy*, which he then dispatched to Bombay, Madras, and Calcutta—

In order to protect American shipping from Algerian corsairs, the U.S. Government issued to merchants this passport to guarantee their vessels safe passage in Mediterranean waters. If an Algerian captain could match his scalloped section of the passport to that of the captain, the ship was unmolested. Other North African pirates, however, continued to prey on the ships.

Salem's Long Reach

Salem's merchant house flags flew in ports in every part of the world, from Lima to Canton, from St. Petersburg to Capetown. So common were Salem's ships in some Eastern ports that traders there regarded Salem as a sovereign nation. During Salem's dominance of the Sumatran pepper trade, the area was called the "Salem East Indies." One key to Salem's success in Eastern markets was the base established by its merchants, especially Elias Hasket Derby, at Isle de France (now Mauritius), 7,000 miles away. From there ships could fan out across the Indian ocean to the Arabian Sea, Bay of Bengal, China Seas, and beyond to the South Pacific.

The travels of *America* in 1804 suggest the scope of Salem's trade. In the spring, *America* returned to Salem from the Indies with spices and pepper. With specie from the sale, she sailed in July to buy Sumatran pepper. She was back in Salem by June of the following year, and immediately sailed for Rotterdam to sell the pepper there for $140,000 in gold, part of which was sent back on another ship. The goods bought in Calcutta with the remaining gold were exchanged in Leghorn for another cargo, which was sold at a great profit in America.

Whampoa Reach was 12 miles downriver from Canton. Foreign captains anchored their vessels here and moved goods to Canton by sampan and junk.

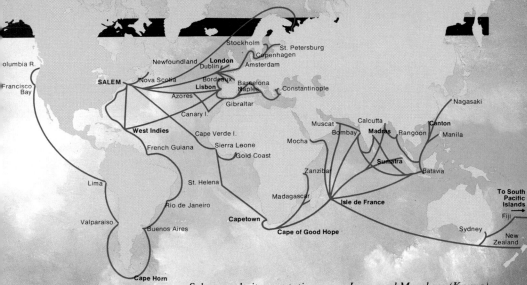

Columbia R.
Francisco Bay
Stockholm
Newfoundland
London
Dublin
Amsterdam
St. Petersburg
Copenhagen
SALEM
Nova Scotia
Bordeaux
Lisbon
Barcelona
Naples
Constantinople
Azores
Gibraltar
Nagasaki
Canary I.
Muscat
Calcutta
Canton
Manila
West Indies
Cape Verde I.
Mocha
Bombay
Madras
Rangoon
French Guiana
Sierra Leone
Gold Coast
Sumatra
Lima
St. Helena
Zanzibar
Batavia
Rio de Janeiro
Madagascar
Isle de France
To South Pacific Islands
Valparaiso
Buenos Aires
Capetown
Cape of Good Hope
Fiji
Sydney
New Zealand

Cape Horn

Salem made its reputation as a small port that opened many foreign markets to U.S. trade: Calcutta, Capetown, Sumatra, Zanzibar, Bombay, Madras, Guam, Madagascar,

Lamu and Mombasa (Kenya), Ceylon, Isle de France, Mocha, Siam, Burma, and St. Helena Island. Salem's main trade routes are shown above.

Where Salem's Ships Called

Martinique, West Indies

Naples, Italy, and the Salem ship Hercules

Gold Coast, Africa, and the Salem brig Herald

Mocha, on the Red Sea

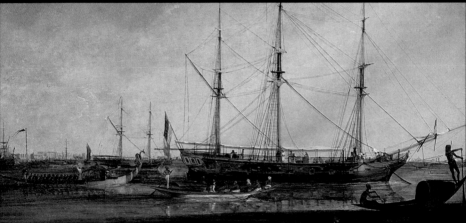

Calcutta, India

Nagasaki, Japan

115

The Goods that Fueled the Trade

More than any other port, Salem was identified with the Eastern luxuries trade. The freighting of necessities was at best a secondary business in Salem. The port's East Indiamen, called "floating bazaars," offered a variety of fine goods bought by the ship-owner for speculation on the world markets. Dozens of goods were handled, but there were trade staples on which the port's prosperity was founded. A Salem ship bound for the East left the

Edw. Halford's fine Virginea
The best in Holbeach for a Guinea.

Among the goods Salem captains obtained with their outward cargoes: tea, sugar, coffee, cotton bandanas, and pepper (**right**).

wharf with West Indies molasses and sugar; European hardware, cheese, and cloth; and American rum, cod **1**, tobacco **2**, barrel staves, butter, beef, and ginseng **3**. The Chinese believed ginseng —"the dose for immortality"

—to be a panacea and aphrodisiac. It was one of the few western products that stirred their interest. They also bought *beche-de-mer* and birds' nests for soup, sandalwood, and mother-of-pearl, which Yankee captains collected from South Pacific Islands. For their goods the captains obtained China tea, Arabian coffee, Sumatran pepper, and Indian sugar and cotton tex-

tiles. Supplementing these typical cargoes were cocoa, spices (cloves, cinnamon, and ginger), ivory, wine, hides, gold dust, and fine silks from China. (Silk-dyeing is shown below.) To their credit, most Salem and Boston merchants and captains shunned the vicious slave trade that enriched several New England ports, but they regarded opium as little worse than rum, and smuggled Turkish and Indian varieties into China.

the first U.S. vessels to visit India. Meanwhile, his father sent *Atlantic* and *Light Horse* to Canton, where they were met by two more Derby vessels, *Astrea* and *Three Sisters*, carrying ginseng their captains hoped to trade for tea. But the price of ginseng had dropped and that of tea risen. To gain more capital, the captains sold *Atlantic* and *Three Sisters* and loaded as much tea as possible on the other two vessels.

It was a good plan, but in their absence the Constitution had been ratified and the new government had established the Customs Service, which assessed the vessels $25,000 in import duties. Unable to pay cash and not wanting to flood the market with over a fourth of the year's supply of tea, Derby successfully petitioned Congress to establish a bonded warehouse system, which would provide free storage for tea in a Customs Service warehouse for up to two years, allowing merchants to pay duties as the goods were sold.

For all the fame of the China tea trade, Canton was a major Salem market for only a few years. It took too long to gather a cargo that would sell in China, and profits were not high enough to justify the cost and risk. Salem merchants after 1790 averaged only one voyage a year to China, and Derby sent no other vessels, preferring to trade with India. Calcutta, Bombay, and Madras became Salem's best Eastern markets, where captains could obtain cotton goods in demand from Manila to New York.

The tea trade was Boston's. The two ports all but divided the East, leaving little to other American ports. Their commercial rivalry circumnavigated the globe, Boston preferring to send its vessels around Cape Horn to the Northwest, where crews obtained furs from Indians before sailing for Canton. Salem vessels rounded the Cape of Good Hope and roamed the Indian Ocean and South Pacific.

In the 1790s, it seemed every other vessel rounding the Cape of Good Hope belonged to Derby or Gray and was commanded by a Crowninshield. From Mocha to Batavia (now Djakarta), Salem vessels were bringing the American flag into Eastern ports for the first time. East India Company officials were dismayed to find their large East Indiamen, owned by a powerful monopoly, often beaten in their traditional markets by smaller ships owned by New

Many American captains and supercargoes preferred to deal with Houqua, the senior hong merchant in Canton and one of the richest men in China. During his long career he proved a steady friend to Americans, who respected him for his fairness and business acumen.

118

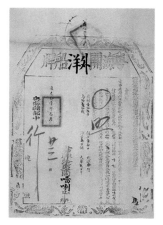

England investors. Able to build and operate a vessel for half of what it cost the British merchant, the newcomers cut deeply into Great Britain's India trade. The Dutch traders in the East Indies resented the Yankees and made them pay their dues. When *Astrea* first arrived at Batavia, supercargo Thomas Perkins was denied permission to do business. It took him a week of wining, dining, and humiliating deference to the Dutch merchants before they deigned to trade with him.

The East became Mecca for every ambitious Salem merchant. The hypothetical voyage in 1803 of an imaginary vessel (called *Junto*) will best illustrate the scope and diversity of Salem's Eastern trade. *Junto* was owned by one merchant, but the venture was ultimately a community effort. The elite Indies commerce was rooted in Salem's less glamorous trades, with each voyage dependent on the numerous schooners and brigs that gathered and distributed cargoes, moving up and down the coast and making trans-Atlantic voyages.

It could take six months to collect the kind of cargo that made such a voyage a good risk. Just as in the 17th century, fish was still the foundation of trade. Cod traded in Baltimore, Alexandria, Charleston, the West Indies, and the Iberian Peninsula brought flour, tobacco, rice, molasses, wine, and salt. To this cargo the owner added New England products—salt beef, butter, and woodenware brought in during the winter on ox-drawn sleds, mast timber, shingles, tar, spermaceti candles from Nantucket, and ginseng. Finally, he loaded $20,000 in hard currency, or specie, packed in small casks.

The owner mapped out a careful trade strategy well before weighing anchor and outlined it to the captain in detailed sailing instructions (here based on actual letters):

Sir: The ship Junto, *being ready for sea, I do advise and order you to come to sail at the first good wind and make the best of your way to Kronstadt* [port for St. Petersburg] *and obtain such items as are demanded in Java. Proceed then to Batavia, and on your arrival there you will dispose of such a part of the cargo as you may think may be most for my interest. If you find the price of sugar to be low, you will then take into the ship as much of the best white kind as will floor her, and fifty thousand weight of*

*pepper; this will store in the fore peak. The sugar
will save the expense of any stone ballast. If prices
for our goods are low, and you have opportunity to
sell the* Junto *at a price that you think will answer,
do it. I would not have you run any great risk as I
shall have little or no insurance.*

Perhaps the greatest source of anxiety for a merchant was being unable to follow the progress of such a voyage, which usually took over a year. Communication was uppermost in merchants' minds: *On your going around the Cape, no doubt you will see some India ships bound for home. You will put letters on two or three of them for me, acquainting me with the situation of the ship, and everything you may think I wish to know.*

In the end, however, all decisions were placed squarely in the hands of the captain. The owner concluded the orders with his customary injunction: *Although I have been a little particular in these orders, I do not mean them as positive and you have leave to break them in any part where you by calculation think it for my interest, excepting your breaking Acts of Trade, which I absolutely forbid.*

Junto, finally loaded, manned, and provisioned, loosed her lines and eased away from the wharf. The owner watched with some apprehension as a good part of his fortune disappeared over the horizon. Many of the crowd of onlookers, cheering as she left, also had more than a passing interest, for on board were their adventures—ginseng, silver, wooden bowls, tobacco, and spice—that the captain would sell or trade to best advantage.

After the captain cleared Salem Harbor and set sail to catch a strong westerly, he retired to his cabin to read over the notes he had taken from the logs in the collection of the East India Marine Society. Observations by other captains on weather and currents and notes on the quirks of certain foreign traders would improve his odds for success.

The first destination was St. Petersburg, where the captain purchased ironware, steel, and zinc needed in Java. Then to London and Cadiz, where he converted his flour, rum, masts, tar, and the rest of his specie to British letters of credit and Spanish dollars, the only western currencies accepted in the East. *Junto* followed the coast of Africa to the Cape of Good Hope and sailed before steady west winds to Isle de France, where the first serious trading would take place. The fate of the entire voyage could be decided there. Fortunately, butter, beef, and shingles were needed, so the captain traded them for sugar, West African cocoa, and casks of olive oil, which the owner's foreign agent said would bring a good price in India. He also noted that candles were in demand in Arabia, so the captain sailed up the African coast on the southwest monsoon, entered the Red Sea, and traded the candles for the famous coffee of Mocha.

He continued this coasting trade around the rim of the Indian ocean: Bombay, along the Malabar coast, Rangoon, buying anything he thought might sell, always trading up. In Madras he took on bandanas, madras, chintz, calico, and seersucker. Finally, *Junto* sailed past Java Head and through the Straits of Sunda. The captain fired a pistol to call for a pilot, who took *Junto* into Batavia harbor. He found coffee, cottons, and metals in great demand, and *Junto* remained in port two weeks while porters carried bags of peppercorns onto the vessel and Malays rowed out their boats full of fruits, crafts, and exotic animals to sell to the Americans.

The hold was still only three-quarters full, so the captain traded his wine for birds' nests and Turkish opium and sailed for Canton. It was a nerve-wracking passage, for the waters were poorly charted, and the Malay Archipelago and the South China Sea were notorious for shoals and deceptive currents. The crewmen literally felt their way through, dropping the lead line constantly to sound the bottom, getting little sleep, keeping the cannon primed to scare off any Malay vessels whose intentions appeared less than honorable. But the fine Hyson tea and the porcelain and silk the captain bought for his wife rounded out the homeward cargo and made the trip worthwhile. Leaving in September, as the monsoon reversed direction, he made good time back to the Cape of Good Hope, where he picked up the southeast trade winds and, with one stop at St. Helena for water, headed home.

Eighteen months after leaving Salem, *Junto* dropped anchor near Winter Island and waited for the customs officer. After inspection, the vessel sailed into the harbor and dock workers, under the wharfmaster's direction, took up the hawsers and slowly warped *Junto* to her berth. Some of *Junto's* pepper and tea would provide cargoes for smaller vessels that would trade it along the coast, starting the cycle over again. Much of it, however, would be reexported to Europe, or even back to the East at a higher profit.

During those years when Salem's Indies commerce was at its peak, pepper was its most profitable cargo, because the port held a virtual monopoly in the spice. Salem owed that to the intuition and good fortune of Capt. Jonathan Carnes. For years, Dutch and British merchants had jealously guarded their Far Eastern sources of black pepper. But while in Sumatra in 1793, Carnes heard rumors of pepper growing wild on the island's northwest coast. Two years later, he left Salem armed with clearance papers showing a false destination for the schooner *Rajah.* For 18 months, *Rajah's* owners waited anxiously while Carnes, and their investment, remained out of touch. On his return he carried the first bulk cargo of pepper imported to America, making a 700-percent profit. Bypassing the Dutch and buying directly from the native merchants, Salem became the center of the world pepper trade until about 1805, when the market was saturated.

The Indies trade was always a risky undertaking. Shipwreck was the greatest fear. Even a grounding in New England waters could bring ruin if the local population plundered the ship. Spoilage was also a constant worry. A voyage to Isle de France took more than 100 days, and the longer the voyage, the more chance that weevils, maggots, rot, mold, or leakage would ruin a cargo. Overzealous captains who broke acts of trade could lose their cargo to a British warship. There was chicanery: A favorite trick in the Philippines was to soak indigo to give it more weight. But Yankees were not above a little sleight of hand themselves, such as passing off New England rum as brandy.

The ever-present danger of pirates in the West Indies, Mediterranean, and, to a lesser extent, in the Far East was a fact of commercial life. Trade was also at the mercy of international politics. A change in relations between European countries could undermine a market on which Salem depended. In a world where there always seemed to be at least two nations at war, Salem vessels were often caught in the crossfire. After only 10 years of peaceful trading

Sewing table brought to Salem from Canton shows fine Chinese lacquer work.

Bringing Home the Exotic

The homes of Salem merchants and captains were graced with artifacts from all over the world. **Clockwise:** *Concentric Balls, carved from one piece of ivory; Fan, with sticks of ivory, sandalwood, tortoise shell, mother-of-pearl, and silver gilt; Chinese Mandarins with nodding heads, clay; Porcelain bowl showing Canton; Chinese Tea Laborers* **(right and left)**, *clay; Chess Pieces, ivory; Silk Robe; Ivory Vase.*

239

Salem captains and crew members often owned tableware printed with the name of their vessel and a standard ship portrait. The print on this pitcher represents Eliza, *a Joseph Peabody ship in the Baltic trade.*

ELIZA

since the Revolution, Salem vessels once again had to dodge privateers when revolutionary France went to war with a coalition of European nations in 1793. So often were Salem vessels condemned and their men impressed that they had to sail in convoy with ships of other neutral nations.

But Napoleon's grand designs helped more than hindered Salem commerce. With European vessels tied up in the conflict, neutral carriers were in great demand to carry food and supplies to the warring nations. The greatly increased tonnage during those years more than compensated for the occasional condemned vessel, and helped make the years between 1790 and 1807 a time of expanding trade and profit—Salem's "Golden Age." Salem by 1804 was in full flower, a prosperous, busy, and elegant port, known for its bold merchants, its domination of the Indies trade, and its handsome Federalist architecture. Most of the 10,000 inhabitants made their living from the sea. Vessels arrived in port at a rate of one a day, and the home fleet had grown to 34 ships, 18 barks, 45 brigs, and 59 schooners, most of which were on voyages, with 48 "round the Cape."

Joining water and shore were more than 30 wharves, crowded with shops, counting houses, and warehouses. Busiest were Union Wharf, bristling with berths; Derby Wharf, the longest in town; and the newest challenger, Crowninshield Wharf. The produce of the world was piled on the wharves and in the warehouses: Cocoa, sugar, molasses, and cotton from the West Indies. Ivory, myrrh, and gold dust from Africa. China tea and silks. Castile soap, wines, figs, lemons, and raisins from Spain. Cinnamon, cloves, nutmeg, and pepper from the Spice Islands. Philippine indigo and African logwood for dyeing. Gin, hemp, nails, and cheese from Amsterdam and Hamburg. Indian cottons, sugar, and cheroots. Prunes and almonds from Marseilles. Muscat coffee, saltpetre, dates, and horses. Russian sail cloth, iron, and cordage.

On old Essex Street, recently paved, were elegant shops, many kept by widows of seafaring men, where one could find English goods, "Yankee notions," India cottons, and other textiles with names like osnaburg, saggathy, and shalloon. The people of Salem were used to seeing exotic peoples strolling their streets, such as visiting Indian merchants with their tall calico headdresses. At the frequent auctions, almost anything could turn up: Arabian camels, tigers, an elephant. But even as the port grew more sophisticated and worldly, Salem acquired something of a reputation for being "unneighborly," and still warned off poor strangers and blacks.

Socially and economically, the city was divided more then ever. Old-line Federalist merchants still lived on Essex Street, but were beginning to build even grander houses on Chestnut Street. This was the western end of town—wealthy and exclusive. To the east, newly-risen Republicans drained and landscaped the old Common and began building their own mansions around it. Below them, nearer the waterfront, were the crowded houses of the sailors, shipyard workers, ropewalk workers, and early Irish and French immigrants. This was the eastern end of town—the nouveau riche, the "common," and the unassimilated.

The geographical split of the town reflected the deep political divisions among the merchants. The New England Federalist party grew out of the post-Revolutionary efforts of merchants to restore the region's shipping economy. Congress repaid their help in getting what Samuel Eliot Morison called the "lawyers' and merchants' Constitution" ratified by passing commercial treaties, offering Federal bounties for fish, and putting heavy tariffs on foreign trading vessels. Within two years the Government was gathering 92 percent of its revenue from shipping duties. The mutually beneficial system brought power to the Federalists, a few of whom, called by their opposition the Essex Junto (from Essex County), ruled Massachusetts and Salem.

Salem's reigning merchant class strove above all for unity in commerce, religion, family, and politics. They perceived a threat to their oligarchy in the growing population of workers and artisans, who found an ally in the Federalists' minority opposition, the Republicans. Domestic politics was only one of the issues dividing the two parties. The almost continuous war between France and Great Britain from 1793 to 1815 was reflected in Salem's ideological battles. The Federalists were pro-British and deeply suspicious of the Revolutionary French. The often younger Jeffersonian Republicans believed that the French were keeping alive the spirit that had won their own independence. Since each of the

The first elephant ever seen in America was brought to Salem in 1795 on the Derby ship America. *The enterprising Capt. Jacob Crowninshield, who paid $450 for the elephant at Isle de France, charged admission at the public showing. The elephant repeatedly shook off a would-be rider, according to Reverend Bentley, and "took bread out of the pockets of the spectators . . . He also drank porter and drew the cork. . . ." Crowninshield eventually sold his prize for $10,000.*

English author Harriet Martineau, visiting in 1834, was impressed by Salem's sophistication:

"Salem, Mass, is a remarkable place. This "city of peace" will be better known hereafter for its commerce than for its witch tragedy. It has a population of fourteen thousand and more wealth in proportion to its population than perhaps any town in the world. . . . These enterprising merchants . . . speak of Fayal and the Azores as if they were close at hand. The fruits of the Mediterranean are on every table. They have a large acquaintance at Cairo. They know Napoleon's grave at St. Helena, and have wild tales to tell of Mozambique and Madagascar, and stores of ivory to show from there. . . . They often slip up the western coast of their two continents, bring furs from the back regions of their own wide land, glance up at the Andes on their return; double Cape Horn, touch at the ports of Brazil and Guiana, look about them in the West Indies, feeling almost at home there, and land some fair morning in Salem and walk home as if they had done nothing remarkable."

warring nations seized American neutral carriers entering the other's ports, Federalists were especially outraged at the French depredations, while Republicans thought the British were the real enemy.

As the split became total, each group huddled in its own social circle. They competed for control of the militia, read different newspapers, attended different churches, danced in different halls, and used different banks. Inevitably, the conflict affected commerce, with partnerships for the most part limited to political allies: the Republican Crowninshields, Hathornes, Silsbees, and Stones; the Federalist Derbys, Ornes, Pickmans, Pickerings, and Forresters. It was a bitter and mean-spirited time, when seamen who did not vote with their employers were blacklisted. William Gray thwarted one plot by his fellow Federalists to ruin the Crowninshields with a boycott. For the Federalists, however, it was a rearguard action. The Republicans slowly but steadily took power. They had the perfect spokesman in the elegant and articulate Jacob Crowninshield. The accumulating bad debts of Elias Hasket Derby, Jr., only reinforced the image of the old guard as the useless rich. Thomas Jefferson's election in 1800 foretold the end of Federalism.

The disunity came at a bad time, for even as Salem continued to enjoy spectacular profits, it was hit with serious setbacks. American vessels venturing into the Mediterranean were increasingly held for ransom by the Barbary pirates, since Algerian corsairs no longer worried about the British warships that had protected colonial shipping before the Revolution. Then in December 1807 came the action that tore apart the once-solid merchant class, marking the turning point in Salem's fortunes. In retaliation for the continuing British and French seizures, Jefferson shut down foreign trade in and out of U.S. ports. The embargo was supposed to force the combatants to recognize the rights of neutral traders by denying American goods to French and British markets. But the inclusion of the Indies and China trades in the ban crippled New England's commerce and undermined Salem's economy.

No one in Salem was neutral about the embargo. Only 25 of Salem's 185 vessels escaped the ban. Firewood could not be brought in, and it was a cold, miserable winter. Federalists like the Derbys and

Joseph Peabody considered independence from the United States preferable to leaving ships idle at the wharves. Federalist New England seriously considered seceding from the Union. The Republican Crowninshields and Federalist-turned-Republican William Gray supported Jefferson and the embargo in spite of the stigma their stand brought on themselves. Federalists labeled them "Jacobins " after the French revolutionary party.

The growing polarization hindered concerted political action in the port's interest. Fortunately, the embargo lasted only 15 months and was lifted in March 1809, the same month James Madison was inaugurated as President. Salem's vessels were soon back at sea, and in the next few years took an even larger share of the Baltic trade. But the port's exports would never again reach preembargo levels. Related industries like shipbuilding, paralyzed during the embargo, were slow to revive. William Gray, Salem's most prosperous and respected merchant before the embargo, was so ostracized for his support of Jefferson that he moved to Boston that spring, taking with him almost a fourth of Salem's overseas commerce.

The embargo divided Salem's merchants as had the Acts of Trade before the Revolution, and again, it was the newly-risen group that prevailed. Of the Salem merchants, only the Crowninshields emerged from those dark days with their fleet and fortune intact. Favoring the new administration and its policies, they picked up where they had left off. The Madison administration, however, did not win over many of Salem's Federalists. Its declaration of war against Britain in June 1812 for "free trade and sailors' rights" was disastrous to foreign commerce, bringing it almost to a standstill. For three years, most vessels lay at anchor under "Madison's nightcaps"—tar buckets over their masts to prevent rotting. Only Salem's anti-British Republicans seriously engaged in privateering against Britain, with the Crowninshields taking the lead. They were the only family to profit from "Mr. Madison's War."

With its fleet cut to 57 vessels—a fourth of its size before the war—Salem found recovery difficult. After the end of the Napoleonic Wars, merchants faced increased competition from French and British shipping—particularly the latter, which picked

Joseph Peabody (1757-1844) rose after the war of 1812 to the position in Salem commerce that Elias Hasket Derby and William Gray had enjoyed in the post-Revolutionary period. From a farm family, he went to sea as a privateer crewman and was captured by the British. He worked his way up to commercial captain and merchant, owning wholly or in part 63 vessels in his lifetime. In the port's declining years he almost single-handedly carried on the Indies trade.

The Customs Service

From his vantage point in the cupola atop the Custom House, the Customs Inspector was one of the first to spot a ship coming into Salem Bay. He immediately was rowed or sailed by a boatman to the quarantine anchorage about 2½ miles out from the port, where he checked the ship's cargo against the captain's manifest, marked and sealed the containers, and gave permission for the vessel to dock. Since 1637, the Customs Service, first Royal and then Federal, had been a strong presence in Salem. When Salem was named one of the 70 original ports-of-entry after independence, the government rented space in several buildings before erecting in 1819 the structure on Derby Street that was used until 1937, when it was incorporated into the National Historic Site.

The Custom House was the focus of Salem's waterfront. Active and retired captains and merchants gathered there for business and gossip; 24 employees registered, inspected, measured, and assessed an average of one vessel a day. In the early years of the nation, 90 percent of the Federal budget came from customs duties, and Salem merchants paid an average of 8 percent of the duties. But these free-wheeling entrepreneurs in the first surge of American capitalism didn't consider it an onerous burden. They even celebrated the formation of the Customs Service, following the ratification of the Constitution in 1788, because they at last had a uniform tax system for all States.

The Customs Service was also one of the earliest regulatory agencies. Collectors managed a fund "for the temporary relief of sick and disabled seamen." Inspectors enforced quarantine and health laws, ensured that there were proper medical facilities on board, and required that each ship carry "60 gallons of water, 100 lbs. salted flesh meat, and 100 lbs. of wholesome ship bread for every person on board." Before other agencies took on the tasks, the Customs Service also handled weights and measures, veterans' benefits, trade statistics, lighthouses, immigration, and search and rescue at sea.

Levying and Collecting Duties

After stevedores had piled a vessel's goods on the wharf, a team of weighers and measurers went to work with scales, dipsticks, and gauges to determine the value of each item. Only the Surveyor was authorized to use the hydrometer to measure the alcoholic content of liquid cargoes. He also issued measurement certificates to captains, registered vessels,

Retired captains often took positions in the Customs Service. Henry Prince, a captain for Elias Hasket Derby, made one of the first American voyages to Manila before retiring around 1800 as a shipowner. He was less than successful, however, and made at least one more voyage before joining the Customs Service as an inspector.

Tools of the trade: *Collector's Office seal, with which customs officers stamped documents; hydrometers used by the Surveyor to measure alcoholic content; lock put on cargo hatch by the Inspector after examining containers; and bung-tapper, below, used to remove stopper from cask.*

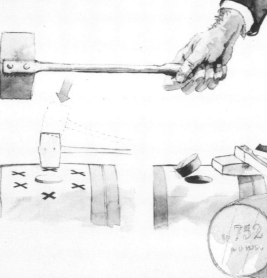

and assessed tonnage duties based on a vessel's carrying capacity. The collection of duties was the job of the Collector, the top official at the Custom House, or his second in command, the Deputy Collector. Duties were levied either by a fixed amount per pound, bushel, ton, etc. (Hyson tea was charged 32¢ a pound in 1793), or by a percentage of the value. (Linens were assessed 5 percent "ad valorem" that year.) The largest duty ever paid on a single cargo was $92,000, assessed on $190,000 worth of China tea and silks brought on the brig *Leander* in 1826.

up much of New England's southern coastal trade after 1815. When New York City gained the edge in the new western markets with the completion of the Erie Canal in 1825, Boston forestalled its own decline by drawing foreign trade away from Salem and Newburyport. Some Salem merchants followed the profits to Boston and New York, strengthening the commercial dominance of those cities.

Infant industries, spurred by the embargoes of 1807 and the War of 1812, were turning the tables. Before the embargoes, industries like distilling served shipping. Now, shipping served the shoe and textile industries. More and more merchants turned from wharf to waterfall, preferring to invest in the burgeoning mill towns of Lawrence and Lowell rather than send their capital to distant markets after scarce commodities. Commerce was giving way to industry, and after the Federalists' unpopular stand against the recent war, they no longer had the influence to guarantee pro-shipping legislation.

The Reverend Bentley witnessed the port's decline during his own final years. He would climb the Crowninshields' stone lookout tower on Winter Island to watch the increasingly rare departures of Indiamen, lamenting in his diary "the stagnation of Commerce." But despite the fading of Salem's glory, the town's slide was not so precipitous as in other small ports. Because its trade was specialized, it was able to hold markets longer. Merchants changed their trade patterns, sending out vessels on shorter voyages, trading cargo for cargo and returning home. They sought new markets: South America, the Maritime Provinces, the South Sea Islands. Salem's final great commerce was on the east coast of Africa— the Zanzibar trade. The gum copal brought from there in 1827 became the port's last trade monopoly.

The merchants also accommodated themselves to the growing Essex County industries, like the Naumkeag Steam Cotton Co. built on the site of Briggs' shipyard. They turned their East Indiamen into "trucks," bringing in raw cotton, hides, gum copal, jute, and wool, and distributing the manufactured textiles, shoes, varnish, burlap, and woolens. But railroads were hurting the coastal trade, and Salem grew less attractive as a port of entry because Boston, a few miles to the south, had better rail connections. In any case, the silting of Salem's already shallow harbor (caused in part by the longer wharves), made it unnavigable for the larger merchantmen and clippers of the mid-to-late 1800s.

The exodus of merchants to Boston and New York quickened as they grew discouraged by stiffening competition. The great dynasties dissolved. But fortunes could still be made in Salem. The popular Joseph Peabody dominated commerce after 1815 as Derby, Gray, and Crowninshield had before him. In his lifetime he owned at least part interest in 63 vessels, sailed by 7,000 seamen. Like the Crowninshields, he made his fortune in the Sumatran pepper trade, and almost alone carried on the China, India, and East Indies trades during Salem's declining years. He was a true philanthropist who sent out some ventures mostly to provide work for Salem's unemployed seamen. When he died in 1844, the port's Indies trade virtually ceased, and Salem was no longer an important port. An observer remarked of Salem and other small New England ports in the following years that they had "the appearance of stillness and retirement; and the inhabitants seem to be separated . . . from all active intercourse with their country."

The return of the schooner *Mattie F.* with a cargo from Cayenne in 1877 brought an end to Salem's era of overseas commercial sail. The harbor remained busy with coastal trade, and Salem vessels continued to freight overseas goods belonging to merchants from other ports, but something was lost. Salem's connection with the East was broken; its ships could no longer be called Indiamen.

Salem's ocean-going sailing vessels established the trade networks that for two centuries were the port's vital arteries. They were also in the vanguard of America's economic and cultural expansion. While explorers on land opened up the continent, maritime merchants, captains, and their crews brought America into the world community. Salem's vessels, opening one port after another to U.S. trade, played a crucial role in the growth of the new nation.

The era of Salem's voyages around the Cape of Good Hope ended in 1870 with the return from Zanzibar of the bark Glide, *owned by Salem's last great merchant, John Bertram.*

Part 3

Salem Then and Now

Visiting Salem Today

With a modern urban community at its back and its wharves stretching far out into Salem Harbor, Salem Maritime National Historic Site is an enclave of the past, a place to recall the years when Salem looked to the sea.

Today this short stretch of waterfront, while lacking the bustle and clutter of the historic maritime period, still looks much as it did 150 years ago. It is an open museum where the stories of the people of Massachusetts Bay's oldest seaport are told through restored and preserved structures. The vital arteries of the port were the wharves, best represented today by Derby Wharf, the longest and one of the most important in Salem. In the counting houses and warehouses on the wharves the merchants made their deals and instructed their captains. The fruits of their labors are apparent in the fine architecture and rich furnishings of the Hawkes and Derby houses, the latter the home of Salem's most prominent merchant. The U.S. Government's presence in Salem was represented by the Custom House, where officials collected duties and performed the dozens of other maritime-associated tasks then assigned to the Customs Service. Restored offices, a slide show, and an exhibit of objects from hardtack to hydrometers explain the workings of maritime commerce and its regulation. A broad array of the types of cargoes brought home by Salem ships can be seen in the U.S. Bonded Warehouse behind the Custom House. A ropemaker— one of the hundreds of people

in Salem who made their living indirectly from the sea— lived in the Narbonne-Hale House. He and other Salem citizens were able to purchase necessities and exotic goods at the West India Goods Store.

The histories of the old waterfront structures are enriched by Salem's other historical resources, such as the Peabody Museum's paintings, models, and artifacts of the sea trade and the elegant merchants' houses overseen by the Essex Institute. Salem Common—Washington Square in the early 19th century—was used in the 17th and 18th centuries for livestock grazing and militia training before becoming the center of a fashionable residential district for merchants. Timothy Pickering, colonel of the militia, was born in the Pickering House, the oldest house in America continuously occupied by the same family. The Old Town Hall was built in 1816 on the site of Elias Hasket Derby's famous mansion. First Church houses the oldest (since 1629) continuous Protestant congregation in America. A pastor of the congregation and namer of Salem, Rev. Francis Higginson, is buried at the Burying Point (the oldest in Salem), as are a passenger on the *Mayflower* and judges in the infamous witch trials. The witchcraft hysteria and trials are explained in a multimedia presentation at the Salem Witch Museum. Chestnut Street, a National Historic Landmark, is one of the most architecturally significant streets in America, with its great Federal-style houses built for Salem's merchants.

The Old Custom House on Central and Essex Streets was the home of the Customs Service from 1805—the year it was built—to 1807 and from 1813 to 1819, when the Custom House was built on Derby Street. The gold eagle, the original of which is in the Essex Institute, is believed to have been carved by Salem architect Samuel McIntire.

Pages 136-137: *Essex Street as it looked in 1830. Houses standing then, such as the Ropes Mansion* (left), *still line the street. The gambrel-roofed, Georgian-style house, built in 1727, was bought in 1768 by the Ropes family, who extensively remodeled the interior. They bequeathed the house to the public in 1907.*

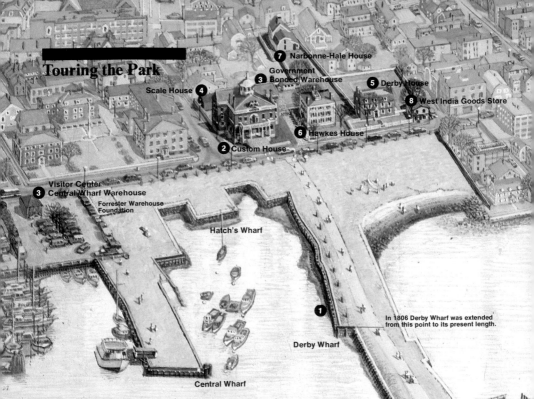

7 Narbonne-Hale House

Government
3 Bonded Warehouse

Scale House **4**

5 Derby House

8 West India Goods Store

6 Hawkes House

2 Custom House

Visitor Center
3 Central Wharf Warehouse

Forrester Warehouse
Foundation

Hatch's Wharf

1

In 1806 Derby Wharf was extended
from this point to its present length.

Derby Wharf

Central Wharf

Salem's waterfront has been greatly altered since the days of its prominence, when more than 30 wharves and dozens of ships lined its shoreline, but the historic site preserves intact an important section of that old waterfront. Its buildings and wharves, most of which date to the port's most prosperous years, formed the heart of historic Salem's commercial district. After the decline of Salem shipping in the late 19th century, the structures were left unprotected and unrestored until 1938, when the area was designated a National Historic Site.

The site is located on Derby Street, Salem, Massachusetts, 20 miles northeast of Boston. Groups may receive special service if advance arrangements are made at the site.
For information write:
Superintendent, Salem Maritime National Historic Site, Custom House, Derby Street, Salem, Mass. 01970.

House of the Seven Gables

Beyond the Waterfront

WINTER

HOWARD

SALEM
COMMON

ST. PETER

CHURCH

TURNER

BRIDGE

Peirce-Nichols House •

FEDERAL

LYNDE

WASHINGTON

ESSEX

11 • 13
10 •• 14
9 • 12

ORANGE

LYNN

NORTH

CARPENTER

Ropes
Mansion •

SUMMER

FRONT

CHARTER

HAWTHORNE

15 •

FLINT

• Assembly House

CAMBRIDGE

NORMAN

DERBY

Salem
Maritime
NHS

CHESTNUT

GEDNEY

SOUTH   RIVER

BROAD

HARBOR

JEFFERSON

CANAL

LAFAYETTE

CONGRESS

9 Peabody Museum
10 Essex Institute
11 John Ward House
12 Gardner-Pingree House

13 Andrew-Safford House
14 Crowninshield-Bentley
House
15 House of the Seven Gables

Lighthouse

1 **The Wharves** remaining in Salem (Derby Wharf, 1762; Central Wharf, 1791; Hatch's Wharf, 1819) represent a fraction of the structures that extended the port's shoreline. Derby Wharf, the longest in Salem, was among those constructed of stone walls and dirt fill. Others were built by floating timber rafts into position, then sinking them with stones. Most of Salem's wharves were lost when the South River was filled in.

Derby Wharf, 1887

Bare now except for the lighthouse, Derby Wharf teemed with commercial life when sailing vessels still unloaded there. Warehouses, workshops, stores, and wagons congested the narrow space. As it was extended and built

1890s

c.1900

up over the years, its appearance constantly changed. Through all the changes, however, it has remained the constant on Salem's waterfront for over 200 years. **Below**: *Derby Wharf in 1910.*

② The Custom House, the Federal-style building in which up to 24 employees of the U.S. Customs Service worked, was built in 1819. On the first floor, the Surveyor's office, the main room where business was transacted, and the steel-doored fireproof vault for records have been restored. Exhibits are displayed in the Deputy Collector's office. The Collector and Naval Officer had offices upstairs, where they could climb to the cupola for a commanding view of the harbor.

The Custom House in 1854

Salem's Famous Son

When Nathaniel Hawthorne faced lean times in 1846, political friends procured for him the position of Customs Surveyor. Salem's commerce had declined by then, and his duties were few: issuing ships' measurement certificates, supervising inspections, and overseeing weighers, gaugers, and boatmen. A contemporary remembered him "mooning about the streets of Salem, a strange and picturesque figure, with gloomy brow and repellent manners." Soon after he lost the position in 1849, he wrote *The Scarlet Letter.* In the introductory essay, "The Custom House," he admitted that his officers, mostly ex-seamen, spent "a good deal of time . . . asleep in their accustomed corners . . . or bor[ing] one another with the several thousandth repetition of old sea stories."

As a boy, Hawthorne handlettered the title page of a ship's log kept by his father, Capt. Nathaniel Hathorne.

144

3 **4** **The Warehouses** were a dominant feature of the Salem waterfront. Crowding the streets and wharves (14 on Derby Wharf), they received teas, spices, coffee, India cottons, and other goods from around the world. Central Wharf Warehouse (1805), which serves as the Visitor Center (right), was typical of the wooden structures along the wharves. A few were of brick, such as Forrester Warehouse (pre-1832—only the foundation remains) and the U.S. Government Bonded Warehouse (1819).

The Scale House (1829) sheltered the large Customs Service scales on which goods landed at Salem were weighed, and taxed accordingly, before they were distributed to domestic markets or reexported. These scales were used in Salem from the 1840s. The scales had to be carried down to the wharves each time a ship arrived. Most ships carried scales similar to these for weighing goods they loaded at foreign ports.

5 **Derby House,** the oldest brick house in Salem, is an excellent example of the colonial Georgian architecture surviving amid the predominant Federal style of the historical port. Merchant Richard Derby built the house in 1762 for his son Elias Hasket. As was the custom, Derby built the house within sight of his wharves and warehouses. (Derby wharf was built in the same year.) A large kitchen was added at the rear of the house around 1790, after Derby had left.

An upstairs bedroom in the Derby House was wallpapered with the printed liners of China tea chests. Silver cruet set was used by the Derby family.

146

❻ The **Hawkes House** was built by Elias Hasket Derby in 1780 to replace his smaller brick residence next door, but he never completed it. The unfinished Georgian mansion was used instead as a warehouse for prize goods taken by his Revolutionary privateers and for trade goods after the war. The original design by Samuel McIntire was altered after the house was purchased in 1800 by Benjamin Hawkes, the owner of a shipyard next to Derby Wharf.

❼ The **Narbonne-Hale House** is one of the oldest houses in Massachusetts. Although it has been somewhat altered, it is still a good example of 17th-century New England architecture. Built as a modest dwelling in 1670, it was later enlarged in a different style. It was inhabited by craftsmen and tradesmen, including a slaughterer and tanner, ropemaker, and cent-shop proprietor. The unrestored house is used in architectural research.

❽ The **West India Goods Store** (c. 1800) was one of many such shops that lined Salem's waterfront in the early 19th century. They provided local citizens with access to the goods landed on Salem's wharves, most of which were destined for domestic markets or reexportation. Capt. Henry Prince, living in E.H. Derby's old house, built the store literally in his front yard to provide his own retail outlet for the goods brought in on his ships, such as molasses, sugar, fruits, china, tea, coffee, textiles, and spices.

9 **The Peabody Museum** is the
oldest continuously operating
museum in the United States.
A maritime museum, it also
houses the country's finest
ethnological collection of
South Pacific and Far East
artifacts. Born in 1799 from
the East India Marine Society's collection of "natural and
artificial curiosities," it was
moved to the new East India
Marine Hall in 1824. It was
renamed the Peabody Mu-
seum in 1867 for philanthropist George Peabody.

The double-stemmed pipe and rhinoceros horn goblet brought from Sumatra by Jonathan Carnes in 1797 were the first objects in the collection that became the Peabody Museum.

Left: *Replica of the salon of George Crowninshield's Cleopatra's Barge.*

10 The **Essex Institute** is one of the oldest independent historical societies in the United States. Founded as the Essex Historical Society in 1821, the Institute documents the story of Essex County, Massachusetts, from 1626 to the present. Phillips Library is a research center for New England and American history. The museum complex includes a gallery of paintings, decorative objects, and domestic artifacts and seven historical houses from colonial times to the Victorian period (following pages).

INDIA SALES,
AT
SALEM.

At the STORE of

E. H. Derby, Esq.

On TUESDAY the FIFTH of APRIL next, at 10 o'clock, A.M. will commence the Sale, by *AUCTION*, of the

Cargo of the Brig Henry,

Lately arrived from *BENGAL, MADRAS,* and *ISLE of FRANCE*; consisting of a large and valuable Assortment of

India Goods,

As follows—viz.

BAFTAS, ⎫ White Cloths, proper
SANNAS, & ⎬ for
CASSAS, ⎭ Shirting or Sheeting.
DUREAS, or striped Muslins.
DUREA CHINTZ, or painted striped ditto.
CHINTZ, a great variety.
STRIPED COTTONS.
JAGRENANT MUSLINS.
Ditto ditto Handkerchiefs.
GINGHAMS.
Blue Cotton HANDKERCHIEFS.
LONG CLOTHS, of a superior quality, suitable for shirting.
MADRAS PATCHES, beautifully

[vertical text: BENGAL.]

Clockwise: *lacquered tea caddy; notice in* Salem Gazette *of India goods auction at Elias Hasket Derby's store; chair designed by Salem architect Samuel McIntire.* **Left**: *Main exhibit hall of Essex Institute.*

151

⓫ John Ward House John Ward was a currier who is believed to have come to America in 1660 when his family fled the plague in England. The Elizabethan dwelling he built on St. Peter Street after 1684 was later enlarged and a second gable was added. After the house passed from the Ward family, it was used as a bakery and tenement before it was acquired by the Essex Institute in 1910, moved to its present location, and restored as a private dwelling.

⓬ Gardner-Pingree House Salem's elegant houses in the Federal style characterize the port's most prosperous era. Perhaps the finest example is the Gardner-Pingree House, built by John Gardner in 1805, and widely admired for its balanced, restrained facade. The massive columns shown opposite adorn the garden side of the

⓭ Andrew-Safford House. Built by merchant John Andrew in 1819, it is the most extravagant architectural display of Salem's commercial wealth.

⓮ Crowninshield-Bentley House For over a century, four generations of Crowninshields lived in this wooden, gambrel-roofed house on Essex Street. Captain John Crowninshield built the house c. 1727-30, before his family became one of the most prominent in Salem. It is an excellent example of a middle-income colonial dwelling. From 1791 to 1819, Rev. William Bentley, well-known scholar and pastor of East Church, rented rooms here from the widow Hannah Crowninshield.

152

15 **The House of the Seven Gables** was built in 1688 by Capt. John Turner. It remained in the Turner family for more than a century before being sold to the Ingersolls. Susannah Ingersoll was a cousin of Nathaniel Hawthorne, who on his frequent visits gathered material for his 1851 novel set in the house.

A Maritime Glossary

Aback: Square sails blown the wrong way on their yards.
Abaft: In the direction of the stern.

Beam: The greatest width of a vessel.
Beat: To tack to windward.
Belaying pins: Wood or metal rods, set free in holes, to which lines are made fast.
Bend: To secure a sail to a yard.
Bilge: Curved part of hull where sides and bottom meet.
Boom: A spar to hold or extend the foot of a sail.
Brace: Line used to swing yard around mast.

Capstan: A vertical winch used to heave anchors or hoist yards.
Close-hauled: Sailing close to the wind.
Close to the wind: As nearly into the wind as possible.
Come about: To turn the ship to bring the wind over the other side.

Deadeye: Circular wooden block pierced with three holes. Lanyard (short line) was threaded, or "rove," through it to tighten the shrouds and backstays.
Draft: Depth of water below the waterline.
Dunnage: Brushwood used to wedge and protect cargo.

Fathom: Six feet of water.
Fid: Hard, tapering pin for separating strands of rope in splicing.
Forecastle: Raised part of deck in the bow. Also crew's quarters belowdecks.
Freeboard: Distance from waterline to upper deck.
Furl: Gather and secure sail tightly to its yard.

Gaff: Angled spar supporting head of fore-and-aft sail.
Gunwales: Upper edge of a ship's side; "gunnels."

Halyard: Line used to hoist or lower sails and spars on mast.
Hawser: Heavy cable for mooring or towing vessel.
Heave to: To swing into the wind to halt vessel.
Heeled over: A ship leaning to one side from the wind.
Helm: Ship's wheel or tiller.
Hogshead: Barrel with capacity of 63 to 140 gallons; liquid measure of 63 gallons.

Kedge: To move ship ahead by pulling on hawser attached to dropped anchor.
Knot: Unit of speed equal to one nautical mile per hour.

Leech: After edge of a fore-and-aft sail.
Leeward: Opposite side from which wind is blowing.
Luff: Leading edge of a fore-and-aft sail. Also, to sail so close to the wind that the luff flutters.

Marling: Binding the end of a rope to prevent fraying.
Marlinspike: Pointed iron instrument for separating strands of rope in splicing or marling.

Nautical mile: 6,080 feet; one minute of latitude.

Oakum: Tarred hemp or jute fiber used to caulk a vessel.
Off the wind: With the wind coming from behind.

Pipe: Wine cask, equal to two hogsheads, or 126 gallons.
Poop: Raised deck at stern.
Port: Left side of vessel. In 18th century called larboard, from "lading board," or loading side.

Quarterdeck: Upper deck aft of the main mast.

Razee: To remove the upper deck from a sailing vessel.
Reach: A tack sailed with the wind coming from abeam.
Reef: Reduce sail area by tying part of it to its yard.
Rope: A stout cord made of twisted plant fiber, especially hemp. Bundles of loose hemp fibers are twisted together into a rough yarn, the basic unit of rope.

Two or more rope yarns are twisted into a strand:

Strands are twisted into various types of rope:

Plain-Laid: Three strands laid right-handed, or "with the sun."

Shroud-Laid: Four strands laid with the sun, over a core.

Cable-Laid: Three plain-laid ropes laid "against the sun."

Run: To sail with the wind.

Scud: To run before the wind, especially when force of wind gives captain no choice.
Sheer: The curve of the upper hull from bow to stern.
Sheet: Line to control the lower corner of a sail.
Shrouds: Lines that give lateral support to mast.
Spar: General term for mast, yard, gaff, sprit, or boom.

For Further Reading

Starboard: Right side of a ship. From "steerboard," the side where rudder was hung on early vessels.

Stays: Fixed lines to support a mast fore and aft.

Strake: One row of planking, stem to stern; "streek."

Studding sails: Extra sails set outside square sails on booms; "stuns'l."

Tack: To sail a zigzag course obliquely opposed to the wind; each course is a tack.

Taffrail: The upper part of a ship's stern.

Ton: A unit of volume; from "tun," a large wine cask with a capacity of 252 gallons.

Tumble-home: The inward slope of a vessel's topsides.

Wales: Thicker and broader strakes on a vessel's sides.

Warp: Move or haul a vessel.

Wear: To change tacks by turning away from the wind and sailing part of a circle until vessel is on new tack.

Windward: "Weather" side, against which wind is blowing. Opposite of leeward.

Yard: Spar crossing a mast, on which square sail is set.

Albion, Robert G., ed., *Naval and Maritime History: An Annotated Bibliography.* Mystic, Conn.: Munson Institute of American Maritime History, 1972.

Albion, Robert G., Baker, William A., and Labaree, Benjamin W., *New England and The Sea.* Middletown, Conn.: Wesleyan University Press, 1972.

Bentley, William, *The Diary of William Bentley, D.D.* (4 volumes). Salem, 1910-14.

Chapelle, Howard I., *The History of American Sailing Ships.* New York: W.W. Norton and Co., Inc., 1935.
____*History of the American Sailing Navy.* New York: W.W. Norton and Co., Inc., 1949.

Crossman, Carl L., *The China Trade.* Princeton: The Pyne Press, 1973.

Endicott, William Crowninshield, *Captain Joseph Peabody,* edited and completed by Whitehill, Walter Muir. Salem: Peabody Museum, 1962.

Felt, Joseph B., *Annals of Salem* (2 volumes). Salem: W. & S.B. Ives, 1849.

Landström, Björn, *The Ship, An Illustrated History.* Garden City, NY: Doubleday and Co., Inc., 1961.

McKey, Richard H., Jr., "Elias Hasket Derby, Merchant of Salem, Massachusetts" (Unpublished dissertation at Clark University, Worcester, Mass.).

Morison, Samuel Eliot, *The Maritime History of Massa-chusetts, 1783-1860.* Boston: Houghton Mifflin, 1921.

Osgood, C.S. and Batchelder, H.M., *Historical Sketch of Salem.* Salem, 1879.

Paine, Ralph D., *The Ships and Sailors of Old Salem.* Boston, 1927.

Peabody, Robert E., *The Log of the Grand Turks.* Boston: Houghton Mifflin, 1926.

Phillips, James D., *Salem in the Seventeenth Century.* Boston and New York: Houghton Mifflin, 1933.
____*Salem in the Eighteenth Century.* Salem: Essex Institute, 1937.
____*Salem and the Indies.* Boston: Houghton Mifflin, 1947.

Putnam, George C., *Salem Vessels and Their Voyages* (4 volumes). Salem, 1925.

Riley, Gaynor R., "The Passing of the Port: Salem in the Nineteenth Century" (Unpublished typescript at Salem Maritime National Historic Site), 1975.

Smith, Philip C.F., *The Frigate Essex Papers.* Salem: Peabody Museum, 1974.

American Neptune, issued quarterly by the Peabody Museum of Salem, and the *Essex Institute Historical Collections,* issued quarterly by the Essex Institute, are excellent sources of information on Salem and its trade. These institutions also hold extensive collections of logs and journals, available to those interested in serious study of Salem and maritime commerce.

Index

Italicized numbers indicate photo, illustration, or map.

National Park Service

All photos, maps, and illustrations not credited here are from the files of Salem Maritime National Historic Site and the National Park Service.

American Antiquarian Society, Worcester, Mass.: 18.
Berry-Hill Galleries, New York: 108.
Boston Public Library: 55 (inset).
British Museum, London: 116 (tobacco trade card).
Ross Chapple: cover photo.
City of Salem: 109.
Essex Institute, Salem: 4-5, 24, 26, 41, 49 (upper portrait), 53, 54-55 (except inset, 55), 65, 88-89, 98 (inset), 124 (ivory vase, left), 126, 132 (portrait), 136-37, 143 (upper right), 144 (logbook), 151.
Fred Freeman (illustrations): 34-35, 140-41.
Greenhorne and O'Mara, Inc.: map, 33.
J. Welles Henderson Collection: 60.

☆GPO: 1986—491-415/40006